Amplified Voices, Intersecting Identities: Volume 1

Mobility Studies and Education

Series Editors

Jane A. Van Galen (*University of Washington, Bothell, USA*)

Editorial Board

Van Dempsey (*School of Education, Health and Human Performance, USA*)
Paula Groves Price (*Washington State University, USA*)
Stephanie Jones (*University of Georgia, USA*)
George W. Noblit (*UNC-Chapel Hill, USA*)
Diane Reay (*University of Cambridge, UK*)
Becky Reed Rosenberg (*UC Santa Cruz, USA*)

VOLUME 6

The titles published in this series are listed at *brill.com/mbse*

Amplified Voices, Intersecting Identities: Volume 1

First-Gen PhDs Navigating Institutional Power

Edited by

Jane A. Van Galen and Jaye Sablan

BRILL
SENSE

LEIDEN | BOSTON

All chapters in this book have undergone peer review.

The Library of Congress Cataloging-in-Publication Data is available online at http://catalog.loc.gov

Typeface for the Latin, Greek, and Cyrillic scripts: "Brill". See and download: brill.com/brill-typeface.

ISSN 2542-8586
ISBN 978-90-04-44511-6 (paperback)
ISBN 978-90-04-39121-5 (hardback)
ISBN 978-90-04-44517-8 (e-book)

Copyright 2021 by Koninklijke Brill NV, Leiden, The Netherlands.
Koninklijke Brill NV incorporates the imprints Brill, Brill Hes & De Graaf, Brill Nijhoff, Brill Rodopi, Brill Sense, Hotei Publishing, mentis Verlag, Verlag Ferdinand Schöningh and Wilhelm Fink Verlag.
All rights reserved. No part of this publication may be reproduced, translated, stored in a retrieval system, or transmitted in any form or by any means, electronic, mechanical, photocopying, recording or otherwise, without prior written permission from the publisher. Requests for re-use and/or translations must be addressed to Koninklijke Brill NV via brill.com or copyright.com.

This book is printed on acid-free paper and produced in a sustainable manner.

Contents

List of Figures VII
Notes on Contributors VIII

Introduction: Amplified Voices, Intersecting Identities: First-Gen PhDs Navigating Institutional Power 1
   Jaye Sablan and Jane A. Van Galen

1 Memories and Migration in Misanthropic Times 16
   Josué López

2 Scenes from the Life of a Burgeoning Mother-Scholar 24
   Becky Morgan

3 A Doctoral Odyssey: Navigating Family, Culture, and Community in a Foreign Land 30
   Travis C. Smith

4 Confessions of a Single Mother in Academia 42
   Araceli Calderón

5 "I Wish Someone Had Told Me It Was Going to Be Like This": Lessons Learned as a PhD Student 49
   Marisa V. Cervantes

6 Black and in Grad School: Demystifying the Intersections of Race and Gender in Higher Education 56
   LaToya W. Brown

7 Locating Struggles with Sociology and Surviving with Mindfulness 60
   Matt Reid

8 From the Mekong and Delaware River to the Merrimack River: The Unintentional Road to the Doctorate 67
   Phitsamay Sychitkokhong Uy and Francine Rudd Coston

9 Enduring: The Misadventures of Navigating a PWI as the Mythical Being Named a Strong Black Woman 74
   Takeshia Pierre

10 Smile Now, Cry Later: Navigating Structures of Inequality in Academia through Resistance, Resilience, and Humor in Our Women of Color Writing Group   82
   Gloria Negrete-Lopez, Lisa S. Palacios and Alejandra I. Ramírez

11 A One-Sided Conversation with Academia   89
   Joy Cobb

12 Just What Is a First-Generation Chinese Male Immigrant and College Student Doing in a *Nice* Field Like Teacher Education?   93
   Lin Wu

13 Strangers Can Make No Noise   101
   Altheria Caldera

14 A Black Girl's Magic Is Often Her Blues   107
   Angela Gay

15 A Particularly Ferocious Fire within Me   114
   Ebony N. Russ

16 This Is Soul Work: A Portrait of Three Black First-Gen Docs   119
   Jason K. Wallace, Raven K. Cokley and Lamesha C. Brown

Index   127

Figures

3.1 Point of no return. 31
3.2 Dark secrets. 32
3.3 A day being black. 33
3.4 Real or fake. 34
3.5 The ancestors. 37
3.6 The ghost of Clemson past. 38
3.7 A true legacy. 39
3.8 Shottas. 40
3.9 The crew. 40
10.1 Left to right: Andrea (facilitator), Lisa, Gloria, and Alejandra. 87

Notes on Contributors

Lamesha C. Brown
(PhD; she/her/hers) is the director of student success/advising at the University of Minnesota Crookston. A recent graduate of the University of Georgia, she became a co-founder of #FirstGenDocs due to her struggles as a first-generation doctoral student and desire to learn more about the experiences of others. Her research interests include: Black women in higher education, first-generation doctoral students, retention and persistence, college access, and diversity and inclusion.

LaToya W. Brown
is a current doctoral student at the University of North Carolina at Greensboro, majoring in Educational Leadership with a concentration in Cultural Foundations. LaToya received her bachelors and master's degrees from North Carolina A&T State University and has worked as an adjunct lecturer for the University in the English and Liberal Studies Departments. Her current research interests include Black feminist theory, Black women and haunting, and social justice.

As a Black first generation college student, LaToya has firsthand experience with learning how to navigate institutional power and has used her work to advocate for minority students in these spaces. She also works to demystify these systems in higher education in her classroom where she teaches students to examine ways in which power, privilege, and injustice operate implicitly and explicitly in schools and society.

Altheria Caldera
is a native Alabamian whose professional and civic work continues the legacy of Black women committed to "lifting as we climb," through education and activism. She is currently a teacher educator in the Curriculum and Instruction department at Texas A&M University-Commerce. The aim of her research and scholarship is to promote educational equity and social justice for students from minoritized backgrounds. She specializes in critical multicultural education, urban education, language identity, and Black girlhood. Dr. Caldera is presently writing a book on Woke Pedagogy.

Araceli Calderón
is originally from Mexico City. She immigrated to the United States at the age of ten. Her mother, a single mother, instilled in her the value of work ethic, which has been fundamental in her life. Two days after her son was born, she went back to school. The act of balancing full-time mothering, full-time work, and full-time

school was challenging; therefore, she sought educational opportunities that were flexible. By the time she was accepted to the PhD program at the University of California, Irvine she had earned two Masters degrees. Because of the demands of the program, her full-time job was replaced with the uncertainty of adjunct positions at local community colleges. After many sacrifices, she became the first person in her immediate and extended family to obtain a PhD in 2019.

Marisa V. Cervantes
is a Latina from the San Francisco Bay Area, is the first in her family to go to college. She attended Loyola Marymount University in Los Angeles, CA where she earned her Bachelor's degree in Sociology and Spanish in 2014. In 2015, Marisa began graduate school at Washington State University where she earned her Master's degree and is now a doctoral candidate in the Department of Sociology.

Her research interests are centered in issues of racial and ethnic identity among Latinx students in predominantly white institutions of higher education. Her previous research focused on intergenerational cycles of domestic violence and violence against women. Marisa teaches sociology classes related to gender, sexuality, and family and serves in advising positions for two undergraduate student organizations. Scholarship, teaching, and service are vital to her personal and professional goals, and she hopes to obtain a position at a teaching university upon completion of her doctoral program.

Joy Cobb
is a third year doctoral student in the Higher Education Administration program at Ohio University. She is also the Enrichment Advisor in the Allen Student Advising Center at Ohio University. Joy has worked in higher education since 2012 and prior to that served 8 years as a high school mathematics teacher. Joy has led multiple presentations focusing on staff and faculty approaches to working with undergraduate students in recruitment and advising.

Joy's current interests include the higher education experiences of first generation and working class students, educational outcomes for students participating on concurrent/dual enrollment, and the consequences of student placement into developmental education. When she is not working with students or preparing for classin the midst of scholarly pursuits, Joy can be found traveling and crafting. Academic pursuits keep her pretty busy, but you can reach her at joydcobb@gmail.com.

Raven K. Cokley
(MEd, NCC; she/her/hers) is a fourth-year doctoral candidate in Counselor Education and Supervision at the University of Georgia. While Raven identifies

as a second-generation college graduate, she became a co-founder of @FirstGenDocs after discovering that her experiences as a Black woman from a single-parent home, mirrored those of her colleagues who were first-generation college graduates. Raven identifies as a first-generation academic, as she will be the first in her family to earn a doctorate. Her research focuses on experiences of high-achievement among Black girls, Black first-generation doctoral students, and Black liberation movements.

Francine Rudd Coston
worked in the Center for Learning and Academic Services as the Coordinator of Transfer Academic Support prior to joining the Office of Multicultural Affairs (OMA) as Associate Director. She was responsible for planning, development and coordination of various academic advising programs, student retention and outreach activities for transfer students. In her current role, she provides support and advocacy to students from diverse backgrounds, religions, culture, as well as the LGBTQ community. Francine received her BS from University of Delaware, in Human Resources and her MA from Rider University in Human Services and Health Administration. Francine is currently finishing her PhD in Leadership in Education at UMass Lowell focusing on first generation transfer students.

Angela Gay
(she/they) is a fat Black cis queer Christian femme womanist, and so much more. She is originally from rural eastern North Carolina and a first-generation college student. They are currently a fourth-year doctoral student studying Educational Leadership, Policy, and Human Development. Her interests center on race and racism in post-secondary education and creating cultures of accountability. During her four years, she has also served, with a full heart, as Assistant Director of the NC State Women's Center, where she teaches, everyone she encounters, to take up space and to use their power to create knowledge(s). Angela is always on a constant journey of learning and unlearning, as taught by the Black feminist tradition and finds their joy and healing in the words of Audre Lorde, magic, intimacy, writing, deep knowing, superhero movies, music, poetry, sweet wine, cupcakes and cheese.

Josué López
is Assistant Professor of Decoloniality and Equity Studies in Teacher Education at the University of Pittsburgh. His research examines the continuity of education for mobile students moving from Central America to the United States. His research explores decolonial approaches to schooling when accounting for transnational mobility under settler colonial rule.

NOTES ON CONTRIBUTORS   XI

Becky Morgan
is a PhD candidate in Clemson University's Educational Leadership, Higher Education program. After growing up in Texas, she attended Wofford College in South Carolina and graduated in 2008 with a BA in English. Following two years of work with AmeriCorps, she returned to the world of Higher Education and graduated from Clemson University in 2013 with her Master's in Counselor Education. She spent the next 5 years serving as the Associate Director for Social Justice Education with Clemson's Harvey and Lucinda Gantt Multicultural Center before entering the PhD program full time.

Gloria Negrete-Lopez
is a Doctoral Candidate in Gender and Women's Studies with a Minor in Mexican American Studies at the University of Arizona.

Lisa S. Palacios
is a Doctoral Candidate in the School of Anthropology at the University of Arizona and tribal archaeological monitor for the Tohono O'odham Nation.

Takeshia Pierre
(MPH) is a first-generation Haitian-American woman in her second year pursuing her PhD in Curriculum and Instruction with a specialization in Science Education at the University of Florida School of Teaching and Learning. Born and raised in Miami, Florida, Takeshia reflects on her experiences with the first-hand educational disparities she's witnessed in the low-income neighborhoods she's lived in and attended during elementary and middle school. She considers her faith, family, and education as the makings of her being, with these three spheres sometimes working together or at odds.

She attributes her lived experiences as a public health practitioner whose worked in community health and her transition to education as the direct influence on her approach for improving science education for underrepresented minoritized (URM) students. Her research centers around socioemotional and resilience training for URM middle school students, STEM mentorship, and culturally responsive pedagogy, framing her studies through a critical race theory lens. Her aim is to provide education that enables URM students to thrive in and outside of school by disrupting barriers and enhancing student identity as learners and doers of science.

Alejandra I. Ramírez
is a Doctoral Candidate at the University of Arizona in Rhetoric, Composition, and the Teaching of English Program, with a minor in Mexican American Studies.

Matt Reid
(PhD) is a graduate of Western Michigan University and assistant professor of sociology at Cabrini University. He has so far had the pleasure of teaching ten different undergraduate courses, including Sociology of Love, Death & Dying, and Social Problems. His dissertation focuses on the experiences of Michigan's medical cannabis patients during a time of emerging legalization. Matt has authored several teaching assignments published through the American Sociological Society and serves as the media editor for the Midwest Sociological Society. He is also the founder of PopularSociology.net, an open-access teaching resource of free video clips that highlight sociology as found in popular media. His hope is to provide instructors with alternatives to the soul-crushing boredom of TED talks and video lectures. Matt currently lives in Kalamazoo with his two cats, Benjy and Rocky.

Ebony Nicole Russ
(MA, MS, ABD) is an award-winning, doctoral candidate in the Department of Sociology and Criminology at Howard University, with concentrations in Medical Sociology and Criminology. Her research interest areas include: health disparities, stress, college student success, cardiovascular diseases, organ transplantation, mental health, domestic violence, policing, and mass incarceration. Ebony has master degrees in both Counseling Psychology and Higher Education and Student Personnel. She previously worked as a clinical therapist with adolescents involved in the Juvenile Justice system and as a Student Affairs professional.

Ebony is a member of the Board of Directors of the Academic Consortium on Criminal Justice Health (ACCJH) and has affiliation with various professional organizations, including the Society for the Study of Social Problems (SSSP), American Society of Criminology (ASC), American Psychological Association (APA), American College Personnel Association (ACPA), Organization of Graduate Sociologists (OGS), Association of Black Cardiologists (ABC), and a proud member of Zeta Phi Beta Sorority, Inc.

Jaye Sablan
(MA) in Feminist Studies, is a genderqueer Indigenous Pacific Islander (Native Chamorro) and is the first in her family to earn undergrad and graduate degrees. She has been working in higher education for 6 years and is the Assistant Director for the University of Washington's Core Programs – Office of Graduate Student Affairs. Jaye's practice-based domains in the field of graduate student affairs are social justice approaches to equity work and holistic student success models. She is also a poet and writer whose work is published in As/Us, Nepantla, Yellow Medicine Review, and Bitch: A Feminist Response to Pop

Culture Magazine. Jaye lives as a humble guest on the lands and waters of the Duwamish people – also known as Seattle.

Travis C. Smith
earned a PhD in the Educational Leadership in Higher Education at Clemson University. As a critical scholar, he focuses on inquiry, practice, and pedagogy that helps disrupt oppressive systems in order to support racially minoritized students. His research agenda is centered in Black student involvement, Historically Black Colleges and Universities (HBCUs), and Black education. Some of his previous work utilizes a variety of methodological qualitative approaches such as phenomenology, photo-elicitation, photovoice, and critical participatory action research. Travis' ultimate goal is to become a university president of a Historically Black College or University (HBCU)

Phitsamay Sychitkokhong Uy
(EdD) is Associate Professor in the College of Education and co-director of the Center for Asian American Studies at University of Massachusetts–Lowell. She has over 20 years of teaching experience ranging from kindergarten to graduate students. Dr. Uy has also worked as a diversity trainer and professional development facilitator for school districts. She is a former secretary of the American Education Research Association (AERA) Research on the Education of Asian Pacific Americans (REAPA SIG) and current associate editor of Journal of Southeast Asian American Education and Advancement. Her research focuses on Southeast Asian American educational experiences and family and community engagement. Dr. Uy is the first Lao American refugee to receive her doctorate from Harvard Graduate School of Education and she is the first tenured Lao American faculty member in a College of Education in the US.

Jane A. Van Galen
is Professor Emeritus of Education at the University of Washington Bothell. Her teaching and research focus on social class and social mobility through education. Most recently, she has focused on ways in which new forms of participatory digital media enable the inclusion of more voices in deliberations about civic and cultural life. She is co-editor of two books on class, mobility, and education: *Trajectories: The Educational and Social Mobility of Education Scholars from Poor and Working Class Background* (Sense Publishers, 2009) and *Late to Class: Schooling and Social Class in the New Economy* (State University of New York Press, 2007). She also edits a book series for Brill | Sense: *Mobility Studies in Education*.

She's the facilitator of the First in Our Families project in which first generation college students create and share digital stories of being First.

Jason K. Wallace
(MEd; he/him/his) is a fourth-year doctoral candidate in the College Student Affairs Administration PhD program at the University of Georgia. Jason is the first in his family to obtain a bachelor's and master's degree and first to pursue a doctorate which sparked his interest in becoming a co-founder for @FirstGenDocs. As a queer Black man from a working-class background, Jason brings a critical and intersectional lens to his scholarship. His research focuses on issues of equity and justice for Black students who hold multiple minoritized identities in higher education.

Lin Wu
was born and raised in mainland China post One Child Policy. He earned his BA in English in China and came to Kentucky to pursue his graduate studies in English in 2006. After earning his master's degree, Lin moved to Tucson, Arizona and started his teaching career in a publicly funded chart school district that serves a predominately working-class Mexican American community. After working in the district for seven years, Lin became a permanent resident of the US.

Lin moved to Seattle in 2015 to pursue his doctorate in Multicultural Education at the University of Washington under the tutelage of Dr. Geneva Gay. His research interests focus on culturally responsive pedagogy, multicultural teacher education, and critical race theory. Lin is currently working as a fulltime instructor in the College of Education at Seattle University and aiming to complete his dissertation by June 2020.

INTRODUCTION

Amplified Voices, Intersecting Identities: First-Gen PhDs Navigating Institutional Power

Jaye Sablan and Jane A. Van Galen

First.

First in their families to finish college. First to go to graduate school. And much too often, the first like them in their graduate school cohorts and the first like them hired in their departments.

In this two-volume project, we merge these personal and institutional layers of being "first" into simultaneous focus. We consider not only the individual trajectories of these authors into the cultural and social spaces of academia in the United States, but also how *they* have borne the burdens of challenging those spaces to be as meritocratic as they claim. The authors of these chapters have navigated deeply unequal systems of education, from childhood through dissertation research, and then into early in academic careers. They have often found themselves unprepared for what was expected of them as they moved through increasingly elite academic spaces. Their institutions have too often been woefully unprepared for people like them.

First-generation Students in College and Graduate School

The contributors to this project have faced formidable odds to even reach graduate school. First-generation students are less likely to have had access to advanced high school coursework, information about academic requirements for college degrees, admissions test preparation, or college counseling while in high school. They are more likely to enroll in two, rather than four-year colleges; first-generation students are four times more likely than peers to leave college after their first year. Nearly half leave college without graduating (Pell, 2011). The authors of these chapters persisted.

Very few first-generation/low-income undergraduates then go on to graduate school (Martin, 2018). While 13% of continuing-generation students go on to attain graduate degrees, only 3% of first-generation students continue through graduate school (Redford et al., 2017).

Once in graduate school first-generation and continuing-generation students may graduate at similar rates in at least some fields (Roksa et al., 2018), but such data masks the formidable differences in the daily experiences between first-generation and continuing-generation students' socialization to the norms and culture of academia. The isolation that many first-generation students experience as undergraduates intensifies as they continue on to graduate school, as academic spaces become even more stratified and competitive and as expectations for success become even more elusive (Ardoin & martinez, 2019; Martin, 2018; Mullins, 2018; Standlee, 2018). The voices in these chapters insist that the obstacles placed in their way be acknowledged and addressed.

These scholars illuminate their embodied experiences of socialization to the professoriate through the lens of such complex intersectional identities as race, ethnicity, gender, sexuality, ability and social class. While the contributors in our texts do not always use intersectionality theory to undergird their narrative pieces and poetry in the formal or explicit sense, all of the contributors make sense of their lives as first-gen doctoral students by highlighting the inter-relationships between their intersecting identities *and* experiences with systems of power and oppression in higher education. Intersectional ways of thinking and being in the world are indebted to the significant scholar-activist contributions of Black feminists such as Kimberlé Crenshaw (who coined the term) (1991), Angela Davis (1983), bell hooks (1981), Patricia Hill Collins (2019) and many more who have not only had a transformative impact across multiple academic disciplines but also across movements for social justice.

Their intersectional first-generation identities bring distinctive perspectives and critique to their scholarship, teaching and service (Hurst & Nenga, 2016; Jones, 2019; Lee, 2017). They may have been among the first of students like them to be visible in their departments, but their departments are now richer for their presence.

Social Class, Intersectional Identities, and First-Generation Students

While each of the authors in these volumes writes from intersecting identities, we distinguish this project from much of the literature on first-generation students by interrogating first-generation status as intertwined with social class – across identities of race, ethnicity, gender, sexuality, and ability.

We want to be clear that we do not claim that social class is the dominant or most important identity for the authors in this project. We acknowledge that intersectional identities cannot so easily be disentangled. We acknowledge, lament, and work to dismantle the deep racism experienced by first-generation students of color. Instead, we consider social-class in this section of our introduction to complicate the prevailing literature on first-generation students. We believe this literature – and broader diversity work on many campuses – will be deepened (and students better served) as it is also better informed by the broader sociological literature on classism, education, and mobility across intersectional identities. Too often in this literature, "class" is simply used synonymously with income.

Within individualistic US culture, social class stratification is often actively denied as a form of structural oppression, even within social-justice activist spaces (Leandor-Wright, 2014). Indeed, US systems of education are deeply rooted in ideologies of meritocracy: anyone with talent and ambition can change classes if only they do well in school. At some level, first-generation students are literally investing years of their lives in this gamble that very high levels of success in school will be rewarded (Jones, 2003; Van Galen, 2010).

Yet optimistic discourse about opportunity through school is rarely matched with analyses of the sorting functions of formal education. Decades of evidence make clear that higher education replicates rather than eradicates class inequalities (e.g. Goldrick-Rab, 2016; Guinier, 2015; Lee, 2016; Mettler, 2014). In the absence of clear public and academic discourse about power, classism, and deep economic inequality, students and their institutions are ill-prepared to provide the ranges of support that would benefit first-generation students. Campuses may celebrate first-generation students' resilience on publicity websites or at commencement, but they too seldom question why the odds were so clearly against these students in the first place.

Much of the literature on first-generation students *does* speak to how financial struggle and uneven academic preparation impede student progress. Yet we argue that social class is ingrained in daily life far beyond income, across intersecting identities. We posit that within daily social interactions, people navigate across and within contested social class hierarchies that are "embodied and turned into a second nature" (Bourdieu, 1990, p. 63), shaping their very sense of themselves and their relative place within the social world. While not all first-generation students are from poor and working-class families, most, by far, are.[1] When first-generation students decide to invest in social class mobility through graduate school, they may anticipate attaining economic security while doing the intellectual work that they love. They may arrive at college being able to at least name the racism, sexism, ableism and homophobia that they'll encounter. They may be less likely to anticipate the "condescension, deference, shame, guilt, envy, resentment, arrogance, contempt, fear and mistrust, or simply mutual incomprehension and avoidance typify relations between people of different classes" (Sayer, 2005, p. 1), even within campus spaces intended to support diverse student identities.

Indeed, the economic homogeneity of communities, neighborhoods, and schools in the US means that college may be among the first settings in which first-generation students have sustained interaction with those of different class backgrounds (and subsequently, the first settings in which more privileged peers and faculty have sustained interaction with less privileged students) (Jones, 2003; Langhout et al., 2007). While many first-generation students begin to recognize their relative economic disadvantage as undergraduates, social class hierarchies become even more apparent in graduate school with even higher concentrations of privileged students and as the norms for success are grounded in ever-more esoteric standards. Economic differences become even more pronounced as graduate students are pressured to limit outside work to demonstrate their full commitments to the life of the mind. Distances between students and their homes and communities grow even wider. As Reay (1997, p. 22) poignantly writes, a source of working-class shame is "a deeply felt sense of working-class inferiority which comes from seeing ourselves through middle-class eyes"; offspring finding success in academia may begin to think, sound, and look to their families like critical middle-class strangers.

Yet little if anything about social class barriers are spoken about in graduate school or new faculty orientations. In part, then, first-generation students face formidable challenges when they pursue class mobility within academic cultures that have not yet fully acknowledged, addressed, or theorized classist policies and practice or the structural obstacles to social mobility (Langhout et al., 2007; Lee, 2017). Decades ago, Sherry Linkon (1999, pp. 2–3) argued that, "the principles of inclusion and recognition that have been so important in creating spaces for gender studies, black studies, queer studies, and ethnic studies [in educational settings] have generally not been extended to class." As bell hooks (1994, p. 177) wrote "nowhere is there a more intense silence about the reality of class differences than in educational settings."

More bluntly, Skeggs (1997) argues that social class is ignored by those with the privilege to ignore it. Decades later, it is rare for scholars to identify their social class origins as they account for how other intersecting positionalities may skew their research or data analysis ("as a white straight male ..."). Social class backgrounds are rarely acknowledged in faculty biographies on department websites or in publications, and are unlikely to be visible without self-identification. Lee (2017, p. 203) writes of how first-generation graduate students and faculty are then stigmatized as colleagues normalize their own privileged experiences and perspectives as widely shared among academics. She describes the "exhausting emotional labor" required of poor and working-class scholars when they have to convince those holding power over them that social class differences do, indeed, matter in navigating the culture and expectations of higher education.

Thus, vulnerable first-generation students and early career faculty often struggle against social class barriers in silence and alone. Few campuses offer workshops for administrators, faculty and staff on identifying classist policies and practice. Privileged students are rarely mentored in (or held accountable for) overcoming their classist assumptions about peers (Langhout et al., 2007; Martin, 2018) though decades of scholarly work documents the pervasive and overt classism that first-generation students encounter throughout their time in school (Gray et al., 2018; Langhout et al., 2007). There are very few social class/class mobility studies departments (and fewer subfields within other academic disciplines to analyze the complexities of class and social mobility across intellectual and professional fields) (Langhout et al., 2007). First-generation students *do* often have the support of excellent Student Affairs' professionals and pipeline programs to help them to navigate academic, social, and financial supports, at least as undergraduates. Yet on most campuses, the "first-generation" identity is framed around "need" rather than as a politicized and agentive intersectional identity entitled to institutional change.

As the "ones who got away" (Reay, 1997) from highly stratified systems of schooling that function to "inscribe failure" (Reay, 2015, p. 21) on poor and working-class students, first-generation students have accomplished far more than many of their peers. And still, success in school may feel precarious. Sayer (2005) argues that the silence, shame and self-doubt that many first-generation students experience is *not* an individual psychological state of "imposter syndrome" but is instead central to how class stratification is sustained:

> Within the educational systems of class societies, the shaming of those who fail is a structurally generated effect, as Bourdieu's extensive research on such systems demonstrates, even though it is felt as an individual failure. (p. 154)

Shame is manifested in multiple ways: In declining to seek help that more privileged students understand as their entitlement; in staying silent in class even when one has the expertise of lived experiences with the issues under discussion; in silently raging at racist and classist and sexist dismissal; in avoiding social situations in which the risk of social "gaffes" is high; in hiding one's background for fear of stigma (Lee, 2017; Rodriguez et al., 2019). The literature on first-generation students speaks often of their "lack" of the cultural capital needed to succeed within the culture of higher education (Mullins, 2018; Portnoi & Kwong, 2011; Ward et al., 2012). This literature is much less clear about why the rules of the high-stakes game cannot simply be explained, or why first-generation students internalize that when the rules remain hidden from them, it's a mark of their own inadequacy.

Within the institution of higher education that was never built for students like them, first-generation students tacitly know that they alone will be blamed if they fall short. As Sayer (2005) elaborates: Those who have invested most deeply in the hope that educational systems are meritocratic may be most vulnerable to shame when they struggle within those systems (p. 154).

In this complicated dance of achievement, doubt, silence, and aspiration, the "'heavy psychic costs" of deeply inequitable systems of education fall on the shoulders of poor and working-class students (Reay, 2015, p. 13). Alison Jaggar (1989) argues that subordinated individuals "pay a disproportionately high price for maintaining the status quo" (p. 166) that requires them to deny their very subordination as a condition of inclusion.

The authors of these chapters speak to all of these things from the intersections of class, race, gender, ethnicity, sexuality, and ability, even when they have not always had access to the analyses that would allow them to frame their experiences as being, in part, manifestations of deeply embodied social class inequality.

Narrative as Critical Reflection

We invited authors to submit critical narratives because of the potential for such writing to add nuance to policy deliberations but also because of the possibilities of critical reflection and identity construction in the work of constructing narratives (Bruner, 1994; Clandinin & Connelly, 1998; Miller, 1994; Ochs & Capps, 2001; Witherell & Noddings, 1991). In constructing narratives, actors do not simply remember, but instead socially create the "perpetually rewritten story" of self (Bruner, 1994, p. 53). Miller (1994) elaborates on narrative as identity construction:

> Remembered details are selected for their perceived effect on an audience, for their fit or challenge to a co-narrator's contribution. Thus, personal stories are not idle tales, whether the issue at hand is self-construction or remembering. Selves, like cultures, are not so much preserved in stories as they are created, reworked, and revised through everyday narrative

practices that are embedded in and responsive to shifting interpersonal conditions. (p. 175)

Written at the crossroads between attaining exceptionally high levels of academic success and having to prove, once again, that they "belong" in faculty roles, these narratives are both a retelling of past experiences and a retelling of the author as a full – and fully critical – member of scholarly communities. At the borderlands of class mobility, these narrators who have embodied class distinctions perform "an evaluation of the self by the self" (Sayer, 2005) in anticipation of others' judgment of them (Skeggs, 1997). Socialized now to the norms of higher education, they reflexively speak back to those who are invested in sustaining those norms. Ochs and Capps (2001) consider the reflective potential of such moments:

> Paradoxically, we are perhaps most intensely cognizant of ourselves when we are unsure of ourselves, including our memories. The tension between certainty and doubt drives narrative activity in pursuit of an authentic remembered self, namely the oscillation between narrators' yearning for coherence of life experience and their yearning for authenticity. (loc 2954)

Indeed, narrative may be vital for reconciling such moments of identity construction (Bruner, 1994; Ochs & Capps, 1996; Vivienne, 2015), particularly for marginalized individuals who rarely have had opportunities to articulate "agentive stances toward their present identities, circumstances, and futures" (Hull & Katz, 2006, p. 44). While there is no shortage of data on the retention and attainment of first-generation students, the students themselves may rarely have had opportunities for "enactment of identity" (Vivienne 2015, loc 687) on their own terms.

Thus, we invited the authors to turn away from the solitary, disembodied academic writing that they've been compelled to adopt to instead to instead write in conversation with one another, through stories, in fiction and poetry, via the visual. They unapologetically write in the languages within which they think and connect to family and community. They write as experts on their own lives and as unique experts on the institutional barriers that exhaust students like them.

As such, these narratives of intersectional identities honor and extend the legacy of first-generation scholar narratives that have so wonderfully amplified the voices of first-generation faculty (Dews & Law, 1995; Housel, 2019; Oldfield & Johnson, 2008; Ryan & Sackrey, 1996; Tokarczyk & Fay, 1993; Van Galen & Dempsey, 2009; Welsch, 2005). Along with the legacy of these earlier voices, these students and scholars decline paternalistic forms of support and instead insist that they be heard as agents of change in higher education. They are transforming pedagogy, creating new forms of scholarship, and deepening research questions. They are strengthening the academy.

The Chapters

In this volume, graduate students write of their socialization to the norms of higher education as they progress through their studies and then dissertation research.

In the second volume, first-generation students write of the early years of their careers as faculty who are establishing themselves as scholars, teachers, and members of their campus communities and professions.

Josué López opens this volume about first-gen college students who are pursuing doctoral degrees with a sense of political urgency. In his essay, he draws connections between anti-immigrant violence in the United States, personal family histories of identity, migration and oppression, and the struggle to earn a doctorate degree – culminating in the philosophical belief that first-gen PhDs often feel an ethical responsibility to create a just and equitable society for historically marginalized communities. Similarly throughout this book, contributors discuss how their various identities based on class, race, gender, and sexuality are shaped by family background, systems of oppression within academia, and a drive to pursue doctoral degrees with the goal of being agents of social change.

In Chapter 2, Becky Morgan offers a glimpse of life as an anti-racist White mother-scholar. She begins by describing a long evening drive home from graduate seminar. Her mind races with many of the anxieties that are familiar to first-gens in doctoral programs; worries about self-competence as well as economic insecurity that stretch back for years. Morgan ends her story by sharing how her partner and sons sustain and ground her, while also showing how she takes an active stance to talk to her children about the social injustices of white supremacy – closing the gap between the Critical Race Theories she learns in graduate school and the everyday.

When first-gen doctoral students of color, and Black graduate students in particular, are on the receiving end of racial micro-aggressions across academia, it can serve as a stark reminder that higher education was not historically built to be inclusive of marginalized communities. In Chapter 3, Travis C. Smith's narrative piece drives this point home by underscoring how a predominantly white university can deploy the rhetoric of "family" to promote a positive and inclusive public-facing image, while in reality, Black working-class graduate students like himself often feel alienated and disconnected from a range of campus-based resources needed in order to thrive.

In Chapters 4 and 5, Araceli Calderón and Marisa V. Cervantes offer individual narratives as Latinas from working poor backgrounds in doctoral programs – with the former being a single mother and the latter as the daughter of a single mother. While asserting that the university as a structure is generally not supportive of single mothers of color, Calderón illuminates the smaller spaces of support within the institution that contributed to her progress. These include faculty who allowed her time away for her studies to take care of her son's needs, dissertation writing groups, and access to fellowships. Cervantes talks about one of the most difficult circumstances to navigate when you're a doctoral student of color who's also first-gen, and that is making the decision to change a primary advisor when you're work and growth as a researcher is not being recognized. While the stakes feel high in this challenging situation, Cervantes draws from family memories of persistence and survival to adapt and pull through.

In Chapter 6, LaToya W. Brown discusses how professors at her undergraduate institution, a Historically Black College and University (HBCU), provided her with the cultural and intellectual support that contributed to her development as a Black, female, and first-generation college student. Brown refers to this support as an ethic of care and found that this was largely absent throughout her experience as a PhD student at a predominantly White institution. From being silenced as a woman of color to feeling like an imposter, she shares strategies that helped her navigate the challenges of being a marginalized first-gen doctoral student.

Matt Reid's story underscores how heterosexism and financial insecurity can negatively impact life as a first-gen PhD student. For Reid, college-educated peers who do not pursue advanced degrees, and who subscribe to heternormative norms, have opportunities to reap the benefits of so-called adult milestones such as working in middle-class jobs, having the capacity to save money, and finally, gaining the ability to purchase homes. This stands in stark contrast to his experience as a working-class White gay man who regularly encounters financial instability as a doctoral student. Like most first-gens, he engages in several piecemeal strategies to try and make ends meet while also making progress towards earning the degree.

Phitsaymay Uy and Francine Rudd Coston, in Chapter 8, share a co-authored piece that illuminates how, in their separate life trajectories, support networks increased their capacities to pursue doctoral degrees. As a Lao American refugee and first-gen whose family experienced the historic trauma of US military violence, Uy acknowledges that while her mother couldn't directly assist with her studies as an adolescent, what her mother could do was connect her with a strong social circle of teachers, neighbors, and community members to advocate for her success. This contributed to Uy's resilience as a doctoral student. Similarly for Coston, as an African American woman and the first in her family to go to college, it was a childhood friend, a high school counselor, and the colleagues in higher education who all motivated her to work towards multiple degrees at the postsecondary and graduate levels.

From Chapters 9 to 11 respectively, first-gen women of color doctoral students highlight strategies to navigate the challenges of being under-represented in academia. For Takeshia Pierre, both spirituality and practicing to let go of the pressure to constantly be the "strong Black woman" helps her cope with the historic and contemporary anti-Black racism embedded in educational institutions where she works and studies. As colleagues at the same institution, Gloria Negrete-Lopez, Lisa S. Palacios and Alejandra I. Ramírez speak back against the institutional racism they experience as Brown and Indigenous people by taking/creating space for a women of color dissertation writing group and by deploying mutually-recognized humor to manage life stressors. Finally, Joy Cobb discusses how she shifted from being unseen in her graduate program as a Black woman from a limited-income background to being able to access opportunities like engaging in research with faculty to responding to call for proposals.

In Chapter 12, Lin Wu shares nuanced examples of his work to practice principles of equity in his role as a Teaching Assistant for a teacher education program at a PWI. As a Chinese immigrant male and first-gen doctoral student, Wu elucidates the challenges and rewards of utilizing social justice theories and pedagogies to engage Master's students in difficult dialogues about white supremacy and racist violence – all the while coping with experiences of institutionalized racism at the individual level.

Altheria Caldera recognizes that while her embodied knowledge as a Southern Black woman who grew up poor is critical to her growth as a scholar in graduate school, she often felt like what James Baldwin referred to as a *suspect-latecomer* – a constant outsider within a largely white cultural sphere. In her narrative, Caldera is forthright about balancing the need to validate the intellectual and professional support she received in her doctoral program on the one hand, while also being authentic about the ways in which whiteness and middle-class culture can police a minitorized graduate student's access to resources and opportunities on the other.

Angela Gay opens Chapter 14 with a powerful poem about survival in a racist, heterosexist, capitalist, and fatphobic world as a Black woman who self-identifies as queer, fat and working-class. Gay then discloses that being in touch with vulnerability allows her to access the strength she needs to traverse everyday experiences with oppression in higher education as a first-gen doctoral student.

In Chapter 15, Ebony N. Russ offers important insights about the intersections of class, race, and gender as it relates to her journey to pursue a PhD as first-gen and a Black woman. First, she shares how her upbringing in a rural, working-class town exposed her to the false idea that "people like her" don't go on to pursue advanced degrees. Second, white male professionals (whether as co-workers or professors), were blatant in their sexist assumptions about Russ's capacity to succeed as a graduate student. Russ persists despite these experiences. Her piece serves as a reminder that while we never truly leave our personal histories behind, these histories can serve as fuel for motivation to succeed. Finally, Jason K. Wallace, Raven K. Cokley and Lamesha C. Brown close this volume by centering the importance and power of community to support and amplify the success of Black first-gen doctoral students. Having recently founded the @FirstGenDocs social media platform, the authors share how developing connections with one another (and a national cadre of peers) have helped them cope and navigate struggles with the complexities, imposter syndrome, feelings of not belonging, and anti-Black racism.

Conclusion

bell hooks (2000) writes of the "price of the ticket" into academia:

> Poor students would be welcome at the best institutions of higher learning only if they were willing to surrender memory, to forget the past, and claim the assimilated present as the only worthwhile and meaningful reality. (pp. 36–37)

In these chapters, these scholars emphatically reclaim memory and refuse assimilation. They decline to perpetuate the myths of meritocracy that serve to reproduce the inequalities of higher education. They are no longer willing to bear the emotional burdens of sustaining the deeply inequitable status quo (Jaggar, 1989).

They ask instead that readers see their agency in building communities that nurtured and sustained them, that readers hear their moments of seething anger. They invite readers to celebrate their moments of triumph after long battles with administrators, as they became deeply invested in their scholarship, and in the class sessions where they spoke up and others finally saw their brilliance. They ask readers to learn from them about teaching students like themselves. These authors insist that readers meet them in their multi-dimensional fullness: the strengths they bring from their families of origin and their own children, their growing strengths as activists, their advocacy for their communities, and their tenacious insistence that they do, indeed "belong" in the academy. Even more importantly, they insist that readers see that the academy needs them.

Note

1 The Postsecondary National Policy Institute reports the median family income for first-year first-generation students is less than half the median family income of first year continuing-generation students (The Postsecondary National Policy Institute, 2018).

References

Ardoin, S., & martinez, b. (2019). *Straddling class in the academy: 26 stories of students, administrators, and faculty from poor and working-class backgrounds and their compelling lessons for higher-education policy and practice.* Stylus.

Bourdieu, P. (1990). *In other words: Essays toward a reflexive sociology.* Stanford University Press.

Bruner, J. (1994). The "remembered" self. In U. Neisser & R. Fivush (Eds.), *The remembering self: Construction and accuracy in the self-narrative.* Cambridge University Press.

Clandinin, D. J., & Connelly, F. M. (1998). Stories to live by: Narrative understanding of school reform. *Curriculum Inquiry, 28*(2), 149–164. https://doi.org/10.1111/0362-6784.00082

Crenshaw, K. W. (1991). Mapping the margins: Intersectionality, identity politics, and violence against women of color. *Stanford Law Review, 43*(6), 1241.

Davis, A. (1983). *Women, race & class* (1st ed.). Vintage Books.

Dews, C. L. B., & Law, C. L. (Eds.). (1995). *This fine place so far from home: Voices of academics from the working class.* Temple University Press; JSTOR. Retrieved from https://www.jstor.org/stable/j.ctt14bswxr

Goldrick-Rab, S. (2016). *Paying the price: College costs, financial aid, and the betrayal of the American dream.* University of Chicago Press.

Gray, B., Johnson, T., Kish-Gephart, J., & Tilton, J. (2018). Identity work by first-generation college students to counteract class-based microaggressions. *Organization Studies, 39*(9), 1227–1250. https://doi.org/10.1177/0170840617736935

Guinier, L. (2015). *The tyranny of the meritocracy: Democratizing higher education in America*. Beacon Press.

Hill Collins, P. (2019). *Intersectionality as critical social theory*. Duke University Press.

hooks, b. (1981). *Ain't I a woman: Black women and feminism*. South End Press.

hooks, b. (1994). *Teaching to transgress: Education as the practice of freedom*. Routledge.

hooks, b. (2000). *Where we stand: Class matters*. Routledge.

Housel, T. H. (Ed.). (2019). *First-generation college student experiences of intersecting marginalities*. Peter Lang Publishing, Inc.

Hull, G. A., & Katz, M. L. (2006). Crafting an agentive self: Case studies of digital storytelling. *Research in the Teaching of English, 41*(1), 43–81.

Hurst, A., & Nenga, S. K. (Eds.). (2016). *Working in class: Recognizing how social class shapes our academic work*. Rowman & Littlefield.

Jaggar, A. M. (1989). Love and knowledge: Emotion in feminist epistemology. *Inquiry, 32*(2), 151–176. https://doi.org/10.1080/00201748908602185

Jones, R. M. (2019). Academic (im)posturing: A critical autoethnography of becoming a Latinx, first-generation college student and professor. In T. H. Housel (Ed.), *First-generation college student experiences of intersecting marginalities* (pp. 89–107). Peter Lang.

Jones, S. J. (2003). Complex subjectivities: Class, ethnicity, and race in women's narratives of upward mobility. *Journal of Social Issues, 59*(4), 803–820. https://doi.org/10.1046/j.0022-4537.2003.00091.x

Langhout, R. D., Rosselli, F., & Feinstein, J. (2007). Assessing classism in academic settings. *Review of Higher Education, 30*(2), 145–179. https://doi.org/10.1353/rhe.2006.0073

Leandor-Wright, B. (2014). *Missing class: Strengthening social movement groups by seeing class cultures*. Cornell University Press.

Lee, E. M. (2016). *Class and campus life: Managing and experiencing inequality at an elite college*. ILR Press.

Lee, E. M. (2017). "Where people like me don't belong": Faculty members from low-socioeconomic-status backgrounds. *Sociology of Education, 90*(3), 197–212. https://doi.org/10.1177/0038040717710495

Linkon, S. L. (1999). Introduction: Teaching working class. In S. L. Linkon (Ed.), *Teaching working class* (pp. 1–11). University of Massachusetts Press.

Martin, J. (2018). The leaky pipeline and lost youth: Why low-income students don't make it to graduate school. In A. R. Standlee (Ed.), *On the borders of the academy: Challenges and strategies for first-generation graduate students and faculty* (pp. 167–192). The Graduate School Press of Syracuse University.

Mettler, S. (2014). *Degrees of inequality: How the politics of higher education sabotaged the American dream*. Basic Books.

Miller, P. J. (1994). Narrative practices: Their role in socialization and self-construction. In N. Ulric & R. Fivush (Eds.), *The remembering self: Construction and accuracy in the self-narrative*. Cambridge University Press.

Mullins, K. (2018). The experience of first-generation, working-class graduate students. In A. R. Standlee (Ed.), *On the borders of the academy: Challenges and strategies for first-generation graduate students and faculty* (pp. 83–101). The Graduate School Press of Syracuse University.

Ochs, E., & Capps, L. (1996). Narrating the self. *Annual Review of Anthropology, 25*, 19.

Ochs, E., & Capps, L. (2001). *Living narrative: Creating lives in everyday storytelling*. Harvard University Press.

Oldfield, K., & Johnson, R. G. (Eds.). (2008). *Resilience: Queer professors from the working class*. State University of New York Press.

Pell Institute. (2011). *Pell institute fact sheet: 6-year degree attainment rates for students enrolled in a post-secondary institution*. The Pell Institute.

Portnoi, L. M., & Kwong, T. M. (2011). Enhancing the academic experiences of first-generation master's students. *Journal of Student Affairs Research and Practice, 48*(4), 411–427. https://doi.org/10.2202/1949-6605.6268

Reay, D. (1997). The double-bind of the "working-class" feminist academic: The success of failure or the failure of success? In P. Mahony & C. Zmroczek (Eds.), *Class matters: "Working-class" women's perspectives on social class* (pp. 18–29). Taylor and Francis.

Reay, D. (2015). Habitus and the psychosocial: Bourdieu with feelings. *Cambridge Journal of Education: Evoking and Provoking Bourdieu in Educational Research, 45*(1), 9–23. https://doi.org/10.1080/0305764X.2014.990420

Redford, J., Hoyer, K. M., & Ralph, J. (2017). *First-generation and continuing-generation college students: A comparison of high school and postsecondary experiences* (p. 27). National Center for Educational Statistics (NCES). Retrieved from https://ies.ed.gov/pubsearch/pubsinfo.asp?pubid=2018009

Rodriguez, M., Hein, S., & Frankel, L. A. (2019). The (im)possible dream. In T. H. Housel (Ed.), *First generation college student experiences of intersecting marginalities* (pp. 51–68). Peter Lang.

Roksa, J., Feldon, D. F., & Maher, M. (2018). First-generation students in pursuit of the PhD: Comparing socialization experiences and outcomes to continuing-generation peers. *The Journal of Higher Education, 89*(5), 728–752. https://doi.org/10.1080/00221546.2018.1435134

Ryan, J., & Sackrey, C. (Eds.). (1996). *Strangers in paradise: Academics from the working class*. University Press of America.

Sayer, A. (2005). *The moral significance of class*. Cambridge University Press.

Skeggs, B. (1997). *Formations of class and gender: Becoming respectable*. Sage.

Standlee, A. R. (2018). *On the borders of the academy: Challenges and strategies for first-generation graduate students and faculty*. The Graduate School Press of Syracuse University.

The Postsecondary National Policy Institute. (2018). *First-generation students – PNPI*. Retrieved from https://pnpi.org/first-generation-students/

Tokarczyk, M. M., & Fay, E. A. (1993). *Working-class women in the academy: Laborers in the knowledge factory*. University of Massachusetts Press.

Van Galen, J. (2010). Class, identity, and teacher education. *The Urban Review, 42*(4), 253–270. https://doi.org/10.1007/s11256-009-0136-z

Van Galen, J., & Dempsey, V. O. (2009). *Trajectories: The social and educational mobility of education scholars from poor and working class backgrounds*. Sense Publishers.

Vivienne, S. (2015). *Digital identity and everyday activism: Sharing private stories with networked publics*. Palgrave Macmillan.

Ward, L., Siegel, M. J., & Davenport, Z. (2012). *First-generation college students: Understanding and improving the experience from recruitment to commencement*. Jossey-Bass. Retrieved from https://ebookcentral.proquest.com/lib/orbis/detail.action?docID=832570

Welsch, K. A. (Ed.). (2005). *Those winter Sundays: Female academics and their working-class parents*. University Press of America.

Witherell, C., & Noddings, N. (1991). *Stories lives tell: Narrative and dialogue in education*. Teachers College Press.

CHAPTER 1

Memories and Migration in Misanthropic Times

Josué López

At the end of 2016, the news mostly forecasted the impending doom that was to come with Trump. Yet no one in my family was naïve enough to think that things were just about to start getting bad for immigrants. Rates of deportation were the highest historically under the Obama Administration so immigrants had been on red alert for a long time. However, that red alert turned into a bloody crimson with Trump.

Over the last couple of years, the images of the Trumpian dystopia occupy every crevice of our cramped living room. Incarcerated children,[1] separated families,[2] the lifeless bodies of immigrants who were murdered after being denied asylum in the United States,[3] families crying because their loved one was murdered by an ICE agent[4] – these play over and over on the news like a highlight reel of pain and suffering. Sometimes we watch and it seems we have lost the words to describe what is happening, or at least to express how we feel about it. How do we remind ourselves that we *are* human beings and deserve to be treated as such when our brothers, sisters, friends, family – all of us – are treated as if we are worthless? White supremacy and colonial domination attempt to choke the humanity out of us so the words get caught in our throat. We are to speak in whispers, a scratch in the back of the throat, barely audible, always hoarse. Struggling. Struggling. Struggling.

However, it is in the struggle itself that we find possibilities. If we are the first-generation of PhDs from historically marginalized communities, then that means we inherit not only the intergenerational agony of generations of oppression, but we also inherit the rich legacy of struggle. It is not possible for us to be here without the work of those that came before us. We may be first generation PhDs, but we certainly are not the first generation to struggle to create a more humanizing reality.

A key resource for our marginalized ancestors, many who gave their lives for the struggle, was a different manner of relating to time. In the act of struggle, past-present-future become one as we think about the responsibility our ancestors left us, our embodied praxis in the present, and the kind of world we wish to leave those that come after us. In this connection between time and struggle, we do not wait idly by for the clock to solve our problems. We work with a different clock that accounts for those that came before us, those that will come after us, and our existence as the embodiment of a then-now.

Thus, *struggle* likely is not a new phenomenon to the first-generation PhD. However, the demands of academic life can introduce a new form of struggle for historically marginalized communities who have been systematically excluded from doctoral studies. How do we make sense of the opportunity and obligation to write, to speak, to act as a first-generation PhD? I provide an answer through two anecdotes during my time as a doctoral student. The first addresses the memories we inherit from elders before they become ancestors. The second point focuses on the way I have addressed immigration not only as an academic challenge, but as a real sociopolitical phenomenon that has severe consequences on our lives. I close by reminding our readers – and also reminding myself – that in these misanthropic times, remembering we continue forward in the path paved for us by our ancestors, and we extend that path for those that will come after us.

Memories

My mother had not seen her mother, my grandmother, in 25 years. We sat on a plane waiting to go to Florida to see my grandmother who had just received her residency. She was staying there with my aunt and cousins rather than coming to the Northeast – where my mom and I live – because it gets too cold for my grandmother.

Borders and dehumanizing immigration politics separated our families for over a quarter of a century. I had only a few memories of who we were together, who we meant to one another. *Family* is such a powerful concept, no doubt about it. But what do you do when you can only understand *family* as an abstract category, as something or someone far away, as a voice on the phone, as a picture in the living room and a story of a time long ago? Could I remember *feeling* something like *family*?

My cousin pulled the car up to the curb as we waited in the arrivals area at the Miami airport. The passenger door opened, and my grandmother slowly shifted her body and her 82-year-old feet to the ground. My mom couldn't wait for her to get balanced, taking her into an embrace that seemed to last a lifetime, or two.

Here, before me, was a 53-year-old child embracing her mother for the first time in over two decades. Tears streamed. Whispers exchanged that no one could hear, but everyone felt what was said. Hair stroked. Faces held. For a moment, it seemed everything stood still.

At that moment, I knew *family.*

One can't help but be infected when that sort of love is present. It spreads, contagious, seeping into every open and bleeding sore that you knew you had – and even into those you didn't. *Family* ceased to be only the idea of family and became *our family.* No longer was *family* just something to muse over. Our family was something to witness, to feel, to remember.

How can we heal wounds created by time lost that we will never get back? I believe part of the answer lies in the memories carried in our stories. I watched my mother and grandmother talk to each other for hours. And I literally mean *hours*. I had to tell my mom on multiple occasions she needed to let Abuela sleep because it was almost midnight and my mom was just getting warmed up. Sometimes my mom listened to me and let her sleep, most of the time she didn't.

Abuela and I also spoke. She told me about her own life growing up in Honduras, born to a Mayan mother that migrated from Mexico and a Black father who migrated from Belize. She spoke of my grandfather, a Mayan man from Copán, Honduras who I never had the chance to meet. He joined the ancestors when my mother was young, drinking himself to death under the weight of reality.

Abuela also told me about my mom, the youngest of nine children. She explained how all of her children had to work instead of attend school, though my mom would sometimes sneak off to go to school anyways because she liked to learn. When my mom was in second grade, Abuela had to show up at the school and physically take her out of the classroom so she could instead go work selling food to neighbors that Abuela would make.

But Abuela would also share the funny and loving stories, too. My mom would spend all night dancing in the club by the beach and Abuela would scold her whenever she came back to the house so late. She also told stories of how she loved being around her children, grandchildren, and great-grandchildren. She would pause when she remembered that now that she was in the United States, she would not see all those kids that have to stay in Honduras because the US government says so. Then, she would turn her body slowly and call one of the grandchildren running around the living room in Miami and hold them with a firm and gentle embrace that could be felt across borders. With a hug she could show that borders do not require us to sacrifice love and happiness; it requires that we re-direct it to fit our situation.

Sometimes our conversations would trail off on long pauses and she would say *oh, I forgot what I was just saying.* Memory is fragile, like the brittle bones that keep Abuela upright.

Yet every time that she was able to retrieve a memory, I held on to it dearly. All these memories served to fill something in my heart that I didn't even realize I had trouble understanding: my mom and I are only the most recent two generations of warriors working to provide those that come after us a better world. We have lost so many people along the way, like my grandfather, who are overwhelmed by the hardships of life and living. Yet we have elder-warriors, like Abuela, who are still with us and want to share their memories. And I also saw my young cousins stumbling through the living room as they learned how to stabilize their legs under them before face-planting on their walking attempts.

In one room, there was the spirit of our ancestors, the wisdom of the elders, the energy of the young, and the hope that comes with seeing children and their potential future. How would I carry these with me when I left? An answer is in the memories, both those shared and entrusted to me by others, as well as those formed in the act of living.

Unfortunately, as first-generation PhD students, we have to confront the fact that these kinds of memories are severely undervalued in academia. These memories gain some legitimacy when they are presented through certain qualitative methods,[5] certainly. These memories certainly gain even more legitimacy when it is a white researcher that extracts the information from a Black or Brown body. However, what if instead of a white researcher, the holder of memories and teller of stories is a Brown or Black son or daughter? These memories gain even more legitimacy if we explain we collected them through *ethnographic* methodology, where we spent months with a people to learn about their experiences. What if instead of ethnographic methodology, though, we talked about this as our life, our embodied experience, and our responsibility to share these stories? What if instead of these memories becoming *data* to fulfill academia's desire to reduce our embodied experiences to empirical evidence, we instead insisted that *memories* and *stories* are the ways those in the present know where we have come from and can imagine where we will go next?

As possessors of memories that recognize our obligations across generations, we can understand that these memories inspire our methodological and disciplinary resistance to the reduction of our experiences to objectified data. Furthermore, these memories can also serve as a source of strength to remind us to go forward. My mom struggled for me, Abuela struggled for her, and we are part of a line of brutalized and enslaved peoples who survived and struggled over five centuries. This produced the possibility of someone like me being a first-generation PhD. These memories are the foundation for a praxis that begins by understanding that those who came before us struggled so that we can be here. It is our responsibility to do the same going forward.

Migration

We can live migration in different ways, and we can also think about immigration in different ways in the academy. Yet, I would suggest that there is something different about thinking and living migration at the same time. When my mother watches the news, she feels immigration at the very core of her being, and it is reflected in her thought. She provides empirical evidence of her own experience crossing the border, engages in comparative analysis between what it was like to migrate in the late 1980s compared to the Trump era, juxtaposes her experiences in Honduras to those in the United States, performs historical analysis from memory to examine how anti-immigrant rhetoric has changed over time. For my mother, an intellectual engagement with questions of immigration is inseparable from her embodied experience.

The same is true for myself. I find myself in a school of education, yet my research focuses on settler colonialism, transnationalism, and the way mobility is limited for Central American migrants. Someone in academia may ask *this doesn't seem very education-centered: Why not do your work in sociology/political science/anthropology/etc.?* It is a deeply frustrating question, but an important question to answer as a first-generation PhD.

My answer is often unsatisfactory to those that defend rigid disciplinary borders. The fact is that migration impacts all facets of our lives: our lawful status in the United States, the way we can/cannot appropriate another culture, whether we choose to assimilate to another culture anyways, social relations in our town/state/country, political possibilities particularly during the Trump era, and even our educational access and opportunities. Consider, for instance, just how many disciplines are implicated in the previous categories – Law, Anthropology, Sociology, Latin American Studies, Indigenous Studies, Black Studies, Cultural Studies, Anthropology, Political Science, and Education, to name a few. The embodied experiences of human beings cannot be understood when intellectual inquiry is limited to a particular discipline.

As first-generation PhDs who know the complexities of embodied oppression, we face a significant disadvantage in this struggle because we become 'legitimate' in a discipline typically by obeying disciplinary boundaries. You are expected to master a specific body of literature, set of terms, concepts, etc., and then you talk to other people who work to understand the world through those particular readings, terms, concepts, etc. Eventually, you become accepted in that community once you demonstrate a strong command of the discourse pertinent to that community and contribute to the canon in some way. As a first-generation PhD, these politics of academia were shocking. Though I am in education, I didn't want my scholarship to follow some narrow and arguably esoteric line of inquiry. Instead, my leading question in research was *what is relevant to the challenges we face, and how might the resources in the academy serve to address such challenges?*

Mobility became key in such efforts. There is certainly human mobility – which people usually refer to as migration – but there are other sorts of mobility that are pertinent to the way I approach my responsibilities as a first-generation PhD. Consider, for instance, the academy does not contain predetermined answers for the challenges we face in our communities. Instead, as an intellectual I begin by gaining a deeper understanding of the struggles our people face and then see the academy as an institution with the resources to support our work in the community. In this sense, the movement between the communities I work with and the academy forms a type of intellectual mobility.

Moreover, the challenges we face in our communities are multifaceted and cannot be easily mapped onto the disciplinary boundaries we tend to obey in the academy. For instance, my work with students in Central America, the United States, and the mobile students who move between these spaces produces questions that cannot be answered by a single discipline alone. My PhD will be granted in Curriculum and Instruction, and there certainly are questions pertinent to the discipline such as *what are effective instructional methods to facilitate learning for mobile students?* However, there are many other questions that cannot be situated specifically in the field: *What is the relationship between social, political, and economic forces that lead to mobility? How do nation-states defend their borders, and how do mobile peoples resist such borders through their mobility? How does the international division of labor contribute to mobility when capitalism is transnational in nature? How do mobile peoples fit into a discourse of settler colonialism and decolonial efforts that defy the border of nation-states and instead imagine open borders in the Western Hemisphere?* To take the experiences of mobile peoples seriously would mean to also take such questions seriously. In order to provide effective analyses and recommendations for moving forward, disciplinary mobility is necessary.

However, one cannot resist disciplinary boundaries alone. Indeed, these boundaries were constructed by a community, so it follows that it will take a community to disrupt them. What I have found valuable for me in this process is reaching out to other scholars, particularly intellectuals committed to imagining another world, whose work defies both the legitimacy of the borders of nation-states as well as the borders between disciplines.[6] These admirable thinkers serve as a source of inspiration for many of us. And like the memories of our ancestors, learning from and working with these intellectuals serves as a source of healing and strength that allow us to go forward.

Conclusion: On Misanthropic Times

Even when I speak to my mother, I have to confront the type of despair that our contemporary immigration politics generate in communities targeted for physical and psychological destruction. She is sad, hurt, afraid. In all honesty, I am too. I am sure we are not the only two.

In these misanthropic times, when we have to begin some conversations by making sure we agree that all people are actually human beings, how do we find strength to go forward? When one is posed as a problem, a drain on society, a subhuman to be feared, exploited, deported, how do we retain our resolve to struggle? As I have offered here, the struggle of the first-generation PhD, I believe, is never one of isolation. We carry the memories of our ancestors and elders with us, as well as the hope we have for those generations that come after us. As first-generation PhDs, we must also insist that we fuse our embodied experiences into our intellectual work regardless of the disciplinary boundaries that contradict such efforts. This, again, we do not have to do alone but rather in community with others that are working towards similar goals as well. It is appropriate to close here with the words of an elder who embodies the messages I attempt to convey here:

> Community does not stop simply at those who stand around us, but also through those who have preceded us. The message from this is that we, too, precede others, and in that regard, we are linked to them if but in the fact that our actions set the conditions for their lives. Implicit in 'us,' then, is a broader 'we.'[7]

Notes

1. Univisión (2019).
2. Telemundo (2019).
3. Univisión (2018).
4. Clarembaux and Cadavid (2018).
5. Gordon (2006).
6. There are numerous scholars to thank for their work and mentorship in my intellectual development such as Eliana Rojas, Xae Reyes, Lewis Gordon, Jane Anna Gordon, Catherine Walsh, and Juan Alejandro Chindoy Chindoy. Such a list is not remotely exhaustive and does not include the numerous graduate students as well as community intellectuals who have also contributed to my formation. And as I know they all would like me to do, I will play the same role for future intellectuals that they have and continue to play for me.
7. Gordon (2006, p. 51).

References

Clarembaux, P., & Cadavid, L. (2018, May 25). *Las dos versiones contradictorias que da la Patrulla Fronteriza sobre la muerte de la joven guatemalteca Claudia Gómez.* Univisión.

Gordon, L. R. (2006). *Disciplinary decadence: Living thought in trying times.* Paradigm Publishers.

Telemundo. (2019, February 11). *Familias separadas en la frontera demandan al gobierno de Trump por el trauma causado.* Noticias Telemundo. https://www.telemundo.com/noticias/noticias-telemundo/familias-separadas-en-la-frontera-demandan-al-gobierno-de-trump-por-el-trauma-causado-tmna3098594

Univisión. (2018, December 20). *Matan de 15 tiros a migrante hondureño que fue deportado tras serle negado el asilo.* Univisión. https://www.univision.com/noticias/inmigracion/matan-de-15-tiros-a-migrante-hondureno-que-fue-deportado-tras-serle-negado-el-asilo

Univisión. (2019, June 25). *Más de 100 niños migrantes son devueltos al centro de detención de Texas denunciado por insalubridad.* Univisión. https://www.univision.com/noticias/inmigracion/vuelven-a-trasladar-a-mas-de-100-ninos-migrantes-a-centro-de-detencion-de-texas-denunciado-por-condiciones-insalubres.

CHAPTER 2

Scenes from the Life of a Burgeoning Mother-Scholar

Becky Morgan

Scene 1

Class ran over again and I'm 30 minutes late for bedtime. I stew in my frustration and guilt for most of the 45-minute drive home. I wish I had known how hard this would be. But then that's been my mantra since I graduated from high school; always feeling unprepared, unaware, isolated, and perpetually learning the hard way. Getting through college was hard enough with the unexpected charges on my student bill, the terms I could never quite catch, the unspoken rules I only learned when I did it wrong and embarrassed myself. I thought by now, having gotten a Master's degree, having worked in Higher Education for 7 years, that this process to a PhD would be easier, smoother. I zip past darkened clumps of trees and farm fields, calculating the hours until I can sleep. At some point tonight I need to:

1. eat
2. spend time with my spouse
3. shower
4. start on the 100 pages and blog post due at 5 pm tomorrow.

Not to mention the coding I need to finish for my assistantship. My life has become a never-ending cycle of read, write, submit, accept shredded submission, repeat. I know that's where the base of my frustration really rests. In my email sits the newest round of feedback on my conference proposal submission. It smells of passive voice. It stinks with unnecessary statements. It reeks of poorly attempted synthesis. Who am I kidding? I'll never be a scholar.

The fog follows me as I slam my car door and trudge to the house.

"Hey, welcome home." His voice is calm, his smile gentle and just like that, the fog dissipates.

"Hey," I reply, dropping my backpack in the doorway and crawling into his lap. I know this place. I know these arms. "How was your night?"

"It was great. Just don't go in the bathroom yet. We had a small debate over splash sizes and the towels are getting the last of it." We both chuckle and shake our heads.

"Are they out?" I look down the hall, listening for any signs of movement. Already I hear quiet giggles and shushing noises.

"Nah, they wanted to wait up for you." My stomach complains loudly and he adds, "why don't you go check on them and I'll warm up some dinner?"

I walk slowly, holding my breath, tip toeing around the squeaky parts of the floor. As I gently push open the door I hear more giggles interspersed with fake snores.

"What's going on in here?" I demand, holding back a smile.

"Mama!" Two heads pop up at once and my stern face cracks.

I lift Sammy from his crib, his chubby fingers gripping the faded pink fox, his head instantly finding the spot between my shoulder and chin. We sit on brother's bed and I take a deep breath of melon-scented ringlets as Charlie wraps long arms around me.

"Mama! We missed you!" he says into my shirt. "Where were you?" The question is so common now, so predictable.

"Well I had class, remember?"

"But why are you soooooo late?" He stretches out the word, practicing his developing exaggeration skills.

"We had a lot to learn about in class so it went a little longer than usual. Hey tell me about your day."

Both voices go at once telling me about the games they played at school, the meal they cooked with Daddy, the splash contest and how the bathroom floor was now covered in suds. As they talk I feel the familiar burn of tears. I always miss so much.

"What did you learn about in class, Mama?" Both faces watch mine as I struggle to reframe my Critical Race Theory class for a two and five-year-old.

"Let's see. We learned about how white people throughout history have hurt People of Color and ways that we can start changing that."[1] Instantly I doubt whether my professor would agree with that summary, the critique of my ability to synthesize still weighing on my mind. *But how much of that doubt comes from my own whiteness? My own privilege?* I find myself falling into the familiar guilt and shame cycle.

"You hurt?" Sammy asks, simultaneously with Charlie's, "why did they do that?" Two sets of eyes watch me, snapping me out of my mental snowball, waiting for answers that I can't, or maybe don't want to shape.

"Let's save that for tomorrow, team," I respond. *Coward*, I tell myself.

"Tomorrow night, can you play basketball before dinner?" Charlie asks. He's been working on his dribbling and always wants a chance to perform.

"I can't tomorrow night, buddy. I have another class."

"Awww ..." The absence of his million-watt smile chills me so I pull him closer.

"It's alright buddy. Why don't I sing you an extra song?"

The trade is agreeable. Children are placed back under covers, kisses shared, animals rearranged. I leave them with a last "good night" and head to the kitchen. *I should have answered them*, I tell myself. I know what I'm talking about. Why can't I just believe that?

The beep of the microwave interrupts my internal rant and I smell pasta sauce.

"Here you go. How was class?" He's standing there in front of a clean sink with a warmed plate of spaghetti in his hands and I don't know if I have ever seen anything more beautiful. We talk about the day and with him, I take the risk and try to articulate all that I learned. He listens, nods, and I feel the doubt disperse for a little while. I really think that's what surprised me the most about this process, mistrusting myself. I've never been an overconfident person but, in the classroom, I used to be a risk taker. The knowledge was worth the difficult process of learning. But this is different. It feels like I'm watching an artist paint a tree. I follow the directions, use the same brushes, the same colors, the same strokes but the moon is too big and the tree's leaves are indistinguishable yellow and orange globs. A PhD isn't about mimicking experts. It's developing your own expertise and speaking from it. I just can't seem to trust my interpretation of the tree.

Scene 2

I feel Charlie's body tensing, tucking tighter to my side as I read the book of poems telling of a father in West Africa in 1753 looking for his son who was kidnapped and sold into slavery.[2] *Maybe I should stop this*, I question for the thousandth time. I glance over at the stack of Pete the Cat books Sammy is building. Those would be more accessible, right? *Who would you be stopping for? Him or you?* Comes the response. With each word I feel as though we're approaching a crossroads that will change us both. Sammy, unable to handle stories with more than 20 words on a page, is getting antsy so I announce the next poem will be the last one tonight. We stop just after Dinga learns that his son, Musafa, was taken.

The book snaps shut in the echoing silence and I wish desperately for the power to read minds. I notice how long his legs are stretched out next to mine. He'll be taller than me by middle school.

"Is it time for songs?" He asks quietly. The crossroads are suddenly before us and it's time to make a choice. I step back.

"Sure. Come on team, let's go do songs." We pass into the next stage of the well-traveled bedtime routine while I stew in my own cowardice. *You know you need to talk about this*, I tell myself, my mind running through all of the articles I've been reading about white students experiencing discomfort to racial awareness. *But he's not a student, he's 5*, I counter. Quotes about the role of exposure[3] in developing white allies start spinning through my head. *You know that talking about this matters.*[4] *You know that white kids only benefit from learning about things like this at early ages*[5] *so why are you stalling?*

My inner debate continues as Sammy turns out the light and we pile on to Charlie's bed for songs. *What would I even say? He doesn't even want to talk about it.* But even as I think it, I know otherwise. He's rearranging his animals for the fourth time. He's stalling. But I can't bring myself to speak. Silence[6] is easier for me, even knowing I'll beat myself up about it later. So I turn us back, avoiding the crossroads, avoiding the truth.

"Mama, why did they take the boy?" His voice is so quiet I almost miss it as I finish Sammy's song request of "Jingle Bell Rock." Just like that, his hand tight in mine, his eyes unblinking, the step is before us.

"Well, the book we are reading is about slavery ..."

"Slavery? What's slavery?" He asks before I can continue.

I take a deep breath, the first shaky step, and we start to talk. I tell him about how white people kidnapped and sold Black people.[7] How people who look like us forced People of Color to work for us, to serve us. He asks questions, forcing me to reframe what I am telling him in words we have in common, words that, in their simplicity, highlight the depth of the atrocity: hate, anger, pain, fear, death.

We sit silently listening to Sammy sing, "twinkle, twinkle, little star," waiting for us to finish.

"Mama, are we bad?" Charlie's large brown eyes, the exact color and shape of my own, look out from under long, dark lashes.

"We? Do you mean white people? Are we bad?" His ringlets bounce around his face as he nods.

Hearing my own fears voiced aloud[8] stuns me.

I allow myself one slow, deep breath.

"I don't think that white people, that we, are bad. But I think that we have done some really bad things. And I think that slavery, though it's over, is still hurting us all today."

"How?"

"White people thought they were better than Black people.[9] We still do. So we changed the world around us so that we can always think we are better than Black people and all People of Color. And because of that we are not kind, we don't share,[10] we hurt people, we don't care for each other the way people should." In the accompanying silence I question every word. "But there are things that we can do now," I add. "We can learn about what white people did in the past and we can change the world by doing better today.[11] We can learn how to be kind, how to share, and how to care for each other. That's something that we can do together."

He stares at his bear for a minute, his fingers drawing circles in the plush fur.

"Can you sing me 'Jet Plane'?"

"Of course, buddy." I wrap him up and his arms circle my neck. I cradle him for a moment like I did when he fit completely in my arms and realize that, this time, we're holding each other.

I started this PhD because I wanted to make change. By investigating the nature of whiteness, the breadth and depth of white supremacy, I wanted to better know myself, my people, and how to build a more just world. But, like all of the other things I didn't know about higher education, I wasn't prepared for the ways it would change me. The internalized lie that racism only hurts People of Color shatters as I hold the burden of whiteness in my arms. I just shared the weight of our history and current reality laden in hate, anger, pain, fear, and death at the hands of us and our people with a five-year-old kid.

As I pull the covers up to his chin, I am convinced he looks older, changed.

"Do you know how much I love you?" I ask. He smiles a little and rolls his eyes.

"Yes," he responds in exasperation. "A whole lot."

"Yep," I affirm with a loud smacking kiss. "All the time, no matter what."

"Hey mama," he asks as I head toward the door.

"Yeah?"

"Can we keep reading that book tomorrow night?" My smile is tight as I struggle to keep the tears at bay.

"Sure. Night buddy."

I leave wondering who led who through the crossroads.

Notes

1 Delgado and Stefancic (2017).
2 McKissack (2011).
3 Cabrera (2012).

4   Robbins (2016).
5   Wolff and Munley (2012).
6   DiAngelo (2012).
7   Hartman (1997).
8   Thompson (2003).
9   Leonardo (2004).
10 Bondi (2012).
11 Cabrera, Watson, and Franklin (2016).

References

Bondi, S. (2012). Whiteness as property: A critical race theory analysis of student affairs preparation. *Journal of Student Affairs Research and Practice, 49*(4), 397–414. https://dx.doi.org/10.1515/jsarp-2012-6381

Cabrera, N. L. (2012). Working through whiteness: White, male college students challenging racism. *The Review of Higher Education, 35*(3), 375–401. https://doi.org/10.1353/rhe.2012.0020

Cabrera, N. L., Watson, J. S., & Franklin, J. D. (2016). Racial arrested development: A critical whiteness analysis of the campus ecology. *Journal of College Student Development, 57*(2), 119–134. https://doi.org/10.1353/csd.2016.0014

Delgado, R., & Stefancic, J. (2017). *Critical race theory: An introduction* (3rd ed.). New York University.

DiAngelo, R. (2012). Nothing to add: A challenge to white silence in racial discussions. *Understanding & Dismantling Privilege, 2*(1), 1–17.

Hartman, S. V. (1997). *Scenes of subjection: Terror, slavery, and self-making in nineteenth century America.* Oxford UP.

Leonardo, Z. (2004). The color of supremacy: Beyond the discourse of white privilege. *Educational Philosophy and Theory, 36*(2), 137–152. 10.1111/j.1469-5812.2004.00057.x

McKissack, P. C. (2011). *Never forgotten.* Schwartz.

Robbins, C. K. (2016). White women, racial, identity, and learning about racism in graduate preparation programs. *Journal of Student Affairs Research and Practice, 53*(3), 256–268. doi:10.1080/19496591.2016.1143834

Thompson, A. (2003). Tiffany, friend of people of color: White investments in antiracism. *International Journal of Qualitative Studies in Education, 16*(1), 7–29. doi:10.1080/0951839032000033509

Wolff, K. E., & Munley, P. H. (2012). Exploring the relationships between white racial consciousness, feminist identity development and family environment for White undergraduate women. *College Student Journal, 46*(2), 283–307.

CHAPTER 3

A Doctoral Odyssey: Navigating Family, Culture, and Community in a Foreign Land

Travis C. Smith

False Narratives

Have you ever wondered what it would feel like to board a spacecraft and be dropped off in an unknown land with no sense of direction or instructions on how to navigate this new terrain? This terrain is a space you do not recognize, with a vibe that is counter-productive – made up of unwelcoming faces with thoughts that were running through their minds saying, "What are you doing here?" This metaphor describes my arrival at Clemson University. This critical narrative will seek to explore my experiences of transitioning to Clemson University as a first-generation Black PhD student using photovoice as a tool to provide visual aids. Photovoice as a methodology foster critical dialogue and about personal issues through photographs and groups discussions. In this essay, photovoice is employed as a form of self-advocacy to call out systemic issues through visual representation.

Before arriving to Clemson University, I did research regarding the campus life and culture of the university. One slogan constantly appeared across the internet: "the Clemson Family." At first look, this slogan resonated with me because family is one of the things I value in life. Growing up poor might have limited me from material things, but it did not prevent me from have a close-knit family. I was also raised in an environment where we considered every community member as part of a larger, collective family in some form or fashion. There were times when your neighbors would feed you, love on you, and discipline you all in one day. To me, family is simply about love, respect, support, and accountability. So when I noticed the Clemson Family slogan I was beyond excited. Unfortunately, I was in for a rude awakening because their slogan did not include me or embody the same meaning as mine.

Determined to meet new people, I set out on a voyage to explore campus. I located the nearest transit bus which ran from my apartment complex to the campus. Ten minutes later I arrived on campus. Eager to meet new people, I said "thank you" to the bus driver and exited the bus. I quickly climbed a mountain of stairs and entered the campus of Clemson University. I explored the campus for the next 60–90 minutes with a goal to meet as many people as possible. However, trying to meet new people was like trying to find a needle in a haystack. I walked around campus acknowledging everyone with a subtle head nod or hand wave. Yet, you would have thought that I was invisible given the responses I received. For the most part, some White students stared at me as if I was a UFO, while other White students simply ignored my presence. Shockingly, some Black students looked me in my eye and turned the other way as if they were afraid to speak to another Black person in public. These interactions remind me of the movie *Get Out* and the peculiar interactions between the Black community members and the main character.

This type of interaction was my first time experiencing subtle racism at Clemson. My undergraduate institution was a Historically Black College/University where a head nod or hand wave was a signal of acknowledgment. Also, the same universal signal (well I thought it was universal) held true at the institution where I received my masters which was a small private predominately White institution. These events puzzled me to my core. Was it something that I was doing? Did the other people on campus know something that I did not know? I did not know what it was but I was determined to figure it out.

As I continued to reflect on this experience, I realized I was presented with this strange energy as I made my way about the campus. This feeling is difficult to explain. It would be as if I am speaking of a spiritual out of body experience. As I reflect, I believe those feelings were the spiritual cries of my ancestors

FIGURE 3.1   Point of no return

warning me of the times ahead. It felt as if I was able to tap into the lost slave souls that were buried throughout campus. This experience reminded me of the biblical story of Cain and Abel and how God heard Abel's blood crying out from the ground. At that moment, I was reminded of the horrific past of Clemson and the physical, mental, and spiritual exploitation of the Black and Brown bodies that lay beneath the foundation of the institution. This was an experience that I will never forget.

Hoping this experience would not repeat itself, I visited campus daily over the next week. Sure enough, the results were the same for the most part every day. These events left me in an unknown mental space. I began to think that something was wrong with me as I internalized these micro-aggressions. My feelings were all over the place from anger, to sadness, to disappointment, to isolation. Out of all the things confused feelings, there was one thing I knew for sure: I was not welcome in this space.

FIGURE 3.2
Dark secrets

FIGURE 3.3
A day being black

The Tipping Point

The next week I decided to stay alone in my tiny house instead of trying to connect with all these strangers on campus. I was exhausted from the previous week of visiting campus everyday search for a sense of belonging. Lucky for me, it was time for class to start at this point. I was excited as I had things to look forward to. I was eager to meet my new professors and begin this journey of the last traditional schooling that I would ever pursue. My class started quite interestingly as my classmates began to introduce themselves by stating their name, hometown, previous occupations, and research interests. I quickly noticed that I was one of two Black students in a class of 16. This was a new experience for me. The class demographics at my both previous institutions where vastly different. My classes at the HBCU I attended were majority Black and the classes at the predominately White institution where I obtained my masters were majority composed of Black students and international students of color. Unfortunately, my racial marginalization would become my norm for the next three years.

As the semester was moving, the time had come for our first doctoral class assignment. At this point, my mind was all over the place. I was having an internal battle with my sanity based on the constant fight with micro-aggressions, isolation, and a lack of sense of belonging. external variables. My thoughts are ranging from isolation in and outside of the classroom to am I smart enough to be here? There was so much happening at one time between the inability to process my mental state to not understanding the class content. I know you might be wondering why I did not ask questions during class. Well, I was simply terrified. I was the youngest student in the class, one of two Black students, had an untraditional trajectory into the field, and I had difficulty articulating my thoughts in a scholarly manner. I recall this thought pattern running through my mind all the time, "they are going to figure out that I am not smart and I

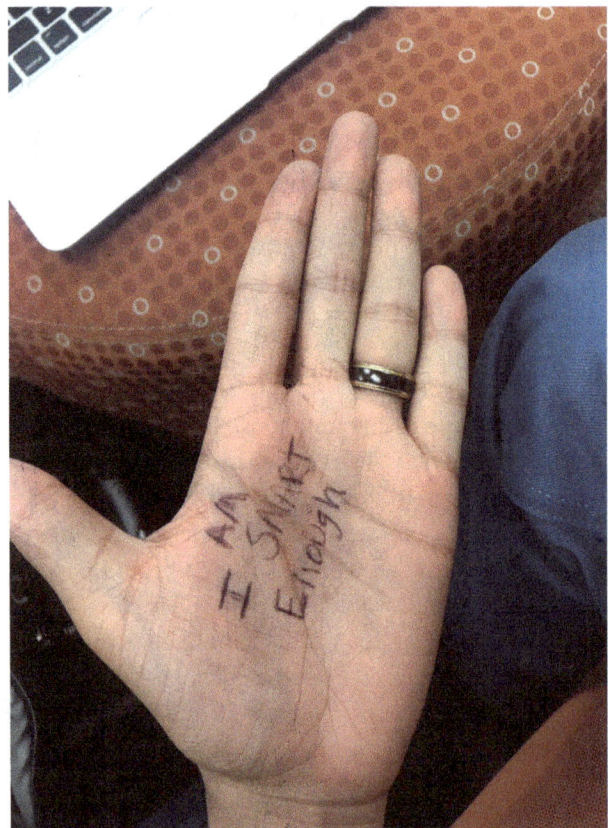

FIGURE 3.4
Real or fake

do not belong here in this doctoral program." It felt as if my White classmates thought little of me as they made statements such as "I would have never known you had a nonprofit," "wow Travis you have done so much" or "good for you." These subtle acts of racism raged me to the core as my beliefs of being an imposter increased. Who would have thought that a 26-year-old man would stoop to such a low perception of himself? Now that I think about it, I was doing exactly what I told my former high school students to never do which was allow outside influences such as stereotypes (Black people are dumb or incapable), micro-aggressions, and subtle acts of racism to determine how you define yourself.

I must admit this was a difficult first semester for me. I found it hard to grapple with understanding epistemologies and ontologies that were discussed in class. I wondered to myself how all of the other students understood the class assignments and the class content so easily. I would soon stumble on the answer. One day after class, I decided to stick around to get a little work done before to make the 45-minute commute back to my tiny home from the satellite campus in Greenville. As I was sitting there, I overheard a couple of my White classmates discussing a folder which they possessed. This folder consisted of previous assignments and reviews for our preliminary exams and was passed down to them. At that moment, I thought my ears were playing tricks on me. Was I hearing correctly?

Sure enough, I heard exactly what I thought and as I looked up the students glanced over at me as if their secret was out the bag. The students approached me and proposed that I study with them to prepare for the preliminary exams. Likewise, I was offered access to the google folder with study materials that were given to them. I was clearly instructed, "do not give anyone else access to this folder." I agreed to their terms (toes crossed) and joined their study group just to get access to that folder and with no intentions of ever attending the study meetings.

The ride home for me was a mental clusterfuck engaging in this interaction. My mind was racing at 1,000,000 miles per minute. I could not come to grips with how I was supposed to feel. My emotions were jumping across the rainbow spectrum from anger to bamboozled to excited. On one hand I was excited to have access to this study folder but on the other hand, I was angry. I felt tricked because all this time I thought I was the slow student for not understanding the class information but the other students had a clear head start with study materials.

I am most furious about not being included in the study folder from the jump and being told not to share it with anyone else. I operated under the assumption we all could receive an A out of the classes so why not help one another. But then I quickly realized this situation was deeper than the eye could perceive. This was one of the first encounters I experienced with being excluded and was a clear example of how majority groups often thrive off of withholding resources from others (racism in academe). As much as I wanted to hide my emotions in a steel safe in my brain, I understood that I would not survive carrying on like that and I had to do something with those feelings.

The Quest

Now with the thought of survival lurking in my brain, I had to create a plan to manage those emotions to create a better mental space for myself. This would be pivotal to my ability to thrive as a doctoral student. I began to think about the previous hardships I faced in my life and how I had overcome them. As I reflected, two notable steps emerged. The first step was the pursuit of knowledge and understanding. I thought back to how I always tried to gain as much knowledge as I could about a given situation which leads to understanding how to navigate and overcome the situation. The second thought that came to mind was a sense of community. I previously mentioned how I thrive when I feel a sense of community and how important it was to me to be immersed in a community that shared similar values. Now knowing these two things, I was able to put a plan into action.

The first part of the plan consisted of the journey to learn as much about Clemson's history as well as the current racial climate and politics of the university. I was assisted with learning about the true history of Clemson by Dr. Rhondda Thomas' Call My Name Project. She presented her research as a guest lecture and campus tour during one of our classes. Her project seeks to uncover the true history of Clemson by telling the stories of the slaves and convict laborers that were used to build the university. As a result of class session, I used my spare time to engage in online learning with her website and other artifacts that illuminated the history of the university. Although this pursuit was extremely triggering at times, it allowed me the opportunity to remove all of the false narratives that were being promoted by the university which created false expectations for students like myself. For example, the board of trustees refer to the integration of Clemson as "Integrating with Dignity," yet the board of trustees and university officials fail to highlight how a lawsuit forced them to integrate. Another example is how the board of trustees and some professors praise Thomas Green Clemson during Legacy Day but fail to mention that he was a slave owner. For me, knowing the truth was liberating and it allowed me to dispel my false historical assumptions of inclusivity, equity, and access for all regarding the university. I was now able to use the

FIGURE 3.5
The ancestors

knowledge to better understand how the university came to be and how its conception still impacts the university today.

The second part of my new plan of survival was finding or creating a sense of community. At first, this task seemed physically impossible as I was seeing hardly anyone who looked like me. This notion would soon change as I met two members of the Black Graduate Student Association (BGSA) named Myrtede and Ashley at an event. If I had to describe them I would refer to them as angels sent from heaven. They quickly took me under their wings and showed me the lay of the land. Ashley and Myrtede introduced me to various stakeholders and decision-makers on campus, mentored me on how to navigate the political and racial scene at Clemson, and also provided opportunities for me to engage with projects across campus such as research groups, special committees, and graduate organizations. As a result of meeting Myrtede and Ashley, I joined a research team that led to conference presentations and publications, I became

FIGURE 3.6 The ghost of Clemson past

Chief of Staff for Graduate Student Government, and I landed a graduate assistantship position in the office of the president.

These opportunities allowed me to thrive at Clemson. I was building my curriculum vitae with the research group while forming relationships across campus with Graduate Student Government. I was getting connected throughout the university and had access to advocate on behalf of other students who looked like me. I knew the right people to approach who had power to implement change. These experiences were eye-opening for me. I finally felt as if I was on a level playing field based on my new network within the university. This expansion of capital opened doors with more opportunities than I could ever imagined. I went on to serve on various campus committees that addressed issues of race and equity, promoted diversity student recruitment, planned and promoted doctoral education for students of color and international diversity.

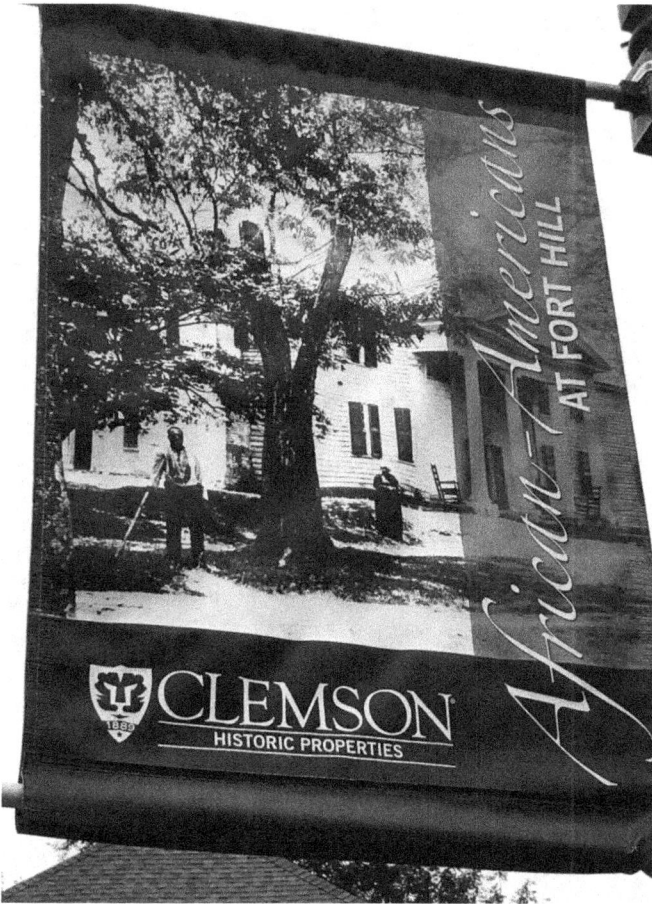

FIGURE 3.7
A true legacy

I give most of the credit to Ashley and Myrtede for their purposeful work in assisting incoming Black graduate students with their transition to campus. Because of these two women, I was able to meet other Black graduate students and create a sense of community here at Clemson. I do not know if I would be the thriving doctoral student that I am if it was not for them taking time aside from their dissertation work to pour into me. Ashley, Myrtede, and BGSA would become an extension to my real family.

At this point, I realized that the "Clemson Family" slogan was a myth for Black people. It probably should be updated and read "Clemson Families" because not everyone is accepted into the larger family. Hence, we have managed to create pockets of smaller families within the Clemson community to survive.

In sum, my experiences helped shaped who I desire to be as an aspiring faculty member within the academy. I hope to be a disruptive force for the systems that limit, discourage, neglect, and exclude person of color. I have

FIGURE 3.8   Shottas

FIGURE 3.9   The crew

accepted the call to fight the good fight in order to open doors for those who are coming after me. I end this essay with my advice to current and incoming doctoral students. Be strong, be you, and be true. No matter how hard the journey is, own and embrace your identities. You can't fit into a system that was not designed for you. I advise you to seek out allies and create a community. Finally, take care of yourself. Be aware of your mental, spiritual, and physical being and protect it at all costs even if it requires choosing another program. Racism will and can kill, so don't sacrifice your life for doctoral degree. In all things just remember we are ONE, "I am because WE are."

CHAPTER 4

Confessions of a Single Mother in Academia

Araceli Calderón

When I was ten years old, my mother brought my siblings and I to the United States. We used to live in *el barrio* where drugs, gangs, death, and poverty were a constant. In addition to working several jobs, my mother (a single-mother) bought a food-truck to generate additional income. Whenever I was not in school, from the age of twelve to seventeen, I was responsible for tending the food-truck. While I sold groceries, drug dealers would sell their drugs on the corner. When cops came into the neighborhood, the dealers would slide by the food-truck (I was inside) and throw their merchandise underneath it as they were fleeing. Later, when the cops were gone, the drug dealers would come back to get their drugs. Needless to say, there were not many educational opportunities in *el barrio*.

Despite not even finishing first grade, my mother knew that education meant success. Thus, she enrolled my siblings and me in educational programs. One summer, when I was in high school, I was chosen to participate in a week-long outreach program at the University of California, Riverside. This life-changing experience was organized by the Migrant Education Program. In retrospect, it was unimaginable that I would earn a post-secondary education, and do so while raising a son on my own. This essay is an account of how my mothering practices intersect with my experiences as a single mother in academia.

Becoming a PhD Student/Candidate

I am the first in my family to obtain a post-secondary degree. By the time I entered the PhD program at University of California, Irvine (UCI) in 2013 I had already earned two Masters degrees, one in Teaching and one in Spanish. As I navigated the different academic spaces I occupied, my mothering practices were not deeply disrupted because I could shift smoothly, and even overlap, between being a mother, an employee, and an academic. My Masters' programs' accessibility (online and late evening classes), the absence of pressure to participate in activities outside of my scheduled classes, and my financial security as a high school teacher translated into an ability to compartmentalize my different responsibilities. I would attend online classes and complete my assignments at night when my son was asleep.

A colleague told me that in order to keep kids out of trouble they should be involved in sports and/or educational programs. That advice made sense to me and I enrolled my young son in activities such as swimming. Unlike other parents that sat at the bleachers and socialized during the two-hour swimming practice, I would spend my time grading papers, having parent conferences, and/or doing academic work. I inherited my mother's work ethic: she always said that with dedication I could achieve anything I set my heart to. When my son was twelve years old, I took a leap of faith and left the security of my job as a high school teacher to pursue a PhD degree. I knew it was not going to be easy, but I was excited to take on the demands of my life as a parent, student, and employee.

The rigors of a PhD program as a single mother (without financial security) were unexpectedly different to my previous experiences as a Masters student. From an institutional perspective, it is assumed that a PhD student/candidate's priorities are first and foremost academic. The holy trinity are considered research, teaching, and service. Personally, this cannot be further from reality. I had to be strategic with my time and finances in order to fulfill my duties as a mother, PhD student, and professional. I have always been the main financial provider for my son. Despite having a financial package, I worked as an adjunct instructor at various nearby community colleges and as a TA in order to make ends meet. I was constantly tired. I remember that every time I would attempt to watch TV with my son, I would fall asleep immediately. Many times my workdays, which included coursework, ran over eighteen hours long. Any alterations to my intersecting identities (mother, student, and/or employee) caused me stress and hindered my performance. On multiple occasions I had to leave the university early because I had to pick up my son when he got sick. I missed important lectures and/or presentations. I had a positive attitude (most of the time) since I realized that my process as a PhD student was beneficial for my son because, through example, I was reinforcing that sacrifices made for higher education are worth it. I will forever cherish the years when my son and I would do our homework together; education united us at a different level.

Although I was proficient at time management and caring for my son, I had concerns about my finances. My financial stability was the marker by which I was measuring my own worth as a mother. My son was entering his teenage years when I started the program and, as always, I wanted to make sure that his needs were met. I reassured myself that if I were able to maintain the lifestyle we had when I was a full–time high school teacher, I could continue thinking of myself as a "good mother." As my son became a young man there was an inevitable shift in my parenting-related demands. He started driving, which meant that I had to pay for driving lessons, a car, and insurance. In addition, the reality of my son's college education was rapidly approaching. I constantly worried about his future, and I would reflect on my commitment to supporting him in his educational path. Just thinking about the cost of putting him through college was stressful. I did not want to take on exorbitant student loan debt because that would prevent me from helping him in his academic journey; therefore, I resolved to continue working at various institutions to pay for my immediate expenses. Because I was going against traditional Mexican norms that recognize mothers as caretakers with no personal aspirations, I felt a disconnect between my desire to grow intellectually and the conventional maternal practices that I felt I was expected to follow. Trying to reach my perceived good mother ideal has been exhausting!

The Institution

Based on my own personal experience as a graduate student, UCI was a place of both anxiety and security. On the one hand, I felt anxious at the end of each quarter/semester when grades were due, when I was preparing for my qualifying exams, and/or when I was unable to attend presentations that were relevant to my research. Before I advanced to candidacy I had no agency over my own time because the institution and the department imposed the academic scheduling. In a given semester/quarter, my schedule consisted of taking two graduate courses, TAing, and teaching three to four courses at different local community colleges. I felt anxious because I wanted to be able to actively participate in more academic activities; however, because of the fixity of the academic schedule, many times this was impossible. Jakobsen et al. (2017) in "Got life? Finding balance and making boundaries in the academy" reveal that institutions prove inadequate to accommodate parents. My experience is that single parents are not fully supported in an academic setting. I felt that my life as an academic was a constant negotiation between my academic and parenting activities.

During the first few years of my program, I regularly questioned my decision to pursue a PhD as a result of the fixed schedules and activities. I continuously felt isolated and stressed. I quickly realized that if I wanted to succeed in the program, I had to use a variety of time management strategies such as Pomodoro and a boot-camp schedule to make sure I could keep up with my academic and personal responsibilities. Both strategies incorporate work segments and breaks, which meant I would do my work (academic and professional) during the work segments, and I would do my personal/maternal labor during the scheduled breaks. I was held accountable and had to meet the demands of my different identities. For instance, as a graduate student, I had to do research, write, and read; as an instructor, I had to answer emails, create and grade assessments, keep student records, and write lesson plans; as a mother, I wanted to spend time with my son and had to cook, clean, and pay bills. The time management and goal-setting techniques I used gave me the necessary structure to be able to manage my different demands.

However, my institution was also a place where I felt a sense of security. UCI was/is a safe space where I felt supported as I advanced as a graduate student. *Money* magazine ranked UCI #1 in the nation on its 2018–2019 list of the nation's "Best colleges" for its support of the diverse student population. Although UCI is advancing in "providing accessible, high quality education and fostering alumni success," I feel that it can be more inclusive of its single-parent graduate students. Even though I felt that there was a lack of support, I was able to find a few programs and groups of people who did help me feel supported. For example, I participated in the Diverse Educational Community and Doctoral Experience (DECADE) program, which provided me with a supportive community. The graduate students that participated in DECADE, like me, were experiencing a feeling of inadequacy because their needs were not being met. I was very lucky because my professors, committee members, and, especially, my advisor were and still are phenomenal in supporting my academic and professional pursuits while being understanding of my demands as a mother. When my advisor and I would meet to discuss my academic progress, first and foremost, she would ask me about my home life. I felt that she validated my role as a mother and a student. The Department of Spanish and Portuguese acknowledged and accepted students' family lives. Some professors organized events (at their houses) for graduate students where children were welcome. My professors were understanding when I missed lectures because I had to tend to my maternal responsibilities. An example of their support was when I had to miss a lecture because my son's high school chemistry teacher told the class – the majority of students were non-Spanish speakers – that the only reason they should learn Spanish was to communicate with dishwashers and cooks. His racist comments were infuriating and it was essential for me to file an official complaint with the high school's Assistant Principal.

Creating and Negotiating My Own Space in Higher Education

The first few years of my doctoral studies were the hardest because I felt a sense of detachment from the institution. To alleviate that feeling, I found allies who supported and guided me in my academic endeavors. Not surprisingly, I found out that there were other PhD students (mothers) negotiating the same institutional adversities as I was. Many single parents, I came to learn, hide their maternal identity in academia because it can be perceived as a limitation in their research program. This omission is often more prevalent for single mothers because the unfair gendered dynamics – which affect women of color at higher rates – still persist in our society. Single mothers' struggles in academia are forced into silence; therefore, they go unnoticed. Unlike some of my colleagues, I embraced and made visible my single-mother status, which allowed me to ask for the support I needed. In order to strengthen my network, I started a dissertation writing group with other women of color and/or single mothers. We supported each other by being accountable to our writing by meeting regularly to work on dissertations and other projects. We felt empowered. The women who consistently participated in the dissertation writing group have suffered in silence the adversities of trying to make ends meet while being a woman of color, and/or a single mother, and a graduate student.

When I was released from my TAing responsibilities the last year of my program, I was able to participate in workshops, presentations, and the graduate student council. I was also selected for the Pedagogical Fellowship, a year-long program for teaching professionalization. I could see the light at the end of the academic tunnel because I could finally devote more time to my academic self. I was making progress to finish my dissertation.

Financial Support

When I advanced to candidacy, the feeling of uncertainty and doubt about my decision to pursue a PhD was assuaged because I regained some control of my own time. My dissertation "Motherhood in Movement: Depictions of the Mexican Revolution (1910–1920) in Literature, Film, and Photography" is directly tied to my personal experiences as a single mother. In my dissertation I analyze how in the early 1900s the national maternal identity of the *mestiza* mother was created in Mexico and the United States through the circulation of various media. I explore three types of unconventional mothers that have been elided from discourses of the Mexican Revolution. First, maternal agents, such as Afro-Mexican mothers and functional mothers, which were women who took care of orphaned children without legally adopting them; second, immigrant mothers to the United States who performed their maternal practices on the road; third, army mothers' resistance from within their home and its effect on how future mothers mothered their children.

As I worked on my dissertation, I applied and was awarded several prestigious fellowships. That financial support allowed me to focus on research and my family. For example, the UC-Mexus dissertation fellowship was transformative because I was able to do research at various prestigious institutions in Mexico such as the Universidad Autónoma de México (UNAM). My son and my mother traveled with me to Mexico City where I had access to archives and met scholars who were fundamental to my academic success. Without the support of the UC-Mexus, I would not have been able to do research outside of my institution. I was also awarded the Association for the Advancement of University Women (AAUW) dissertation completion fellowship. Upon receiving the AAUW, I was released from my TAing responsibilities at my home institution during the last year of my program, which was essential for me to finish my dissertation in a timely manner. Having some agency over my own time and accessing additional financial support gave me the freedom to transition more smoothly between my shifting identities. I am humbled and very grateful for the financial and academic support I have received. I came to appreciate and value our historical interconnectedness to the many men and women who have paved the way for equality for female academics.

Inherited Precepts

Throughout the years of my doctoral studies, I felt that I was being evaluated on the quality of my mothering practices, the quality of my academic work, and the quality of my performance as an employee. My maternal performance was validated when my friends would make comments such as "when I have a child I want him to be like your son." As an academic my recognition was based on the grants and fellowships I received. As an employee I received positive student evaluations and favorable end-of-the-semester observations from administrators. I am grateful for having an opportunity to achieve the highest educational level, especially because my son has been supportive by being a "good" child. I realize the irony (and problem) of speaking of him in this way. I am now evaluating my son's performance through two filters: first, through my own perception of what a "good" son ought to be, and second, through other people's perception that a "good" mother is based on their child's behavior. He has made positive decisions that influence how I navigate my different intersecting and conflicting identities. My graduate work, mothering practices, and employment have been easier because of our good relationship.

Conclusion

I had to put in a lot of work, effort, and dedication to attain my PhD. Being a first-generation Latina single mother in graduate school has had many bittersweet moments. However, I want to finalize this account of my journey on two positive notes. First, my son achieved a level of maturity at a very early age; he has always been inquisitive, and I have pushed his critical thinking skills. I have taught him to articulate his thoughts and to express his opinions in order to have meaningful discussions in which he can grow and continue learning. This was possible because of my own evolution as an academic. Second, I would not be the first in my community to achieve the highest educational level if I had not been supported by my family, friends, professors, and mentors. Having a strong support network was essential for my success. When the abstract for this piece was accepted, I was approaching the finish line of my PhD journey. During my graduation ceremony, as I walked to the stage, I could not help but to think of how my pursuit of a PhD has impacted many people in my life. I shared with my students my process as a PhD candidate, and they were able to see that it is possible for them to reach the highest level of education. I supported my friends by mentoring them on how to navigate the education system so that their children could pursue a post-secondary education. Of my siblings I am the only college graduate; however, most of my nieces and nephews – firs-generation Latin@s – have obtained college degrees. My son is a second-generation student at Cal State University, Fullerton where he is pursuing a degree in Computer Science.

Friends, students, and family were present at my graduation. As I saw their proud faces, especially my mother's and my son's, the mixed emotions of the doctoral process were replaced with a genuine feeling of fulfillment. At last, I was walking to the stage to be hooded. I am a Latina single mother PhD ¡Sí se puede! ¡She sí puede!

References

Jakobsen, J. R., Ott, K., McGinley, D., Smith, A., & Highbaugh, C. A. (2017, Fall). Got life? Finding balance and making boundaries in the academy. *Journal of Feminist Studies in Religion*, 23(2), 127–148.

University of California-Irvine is #1 on MONEY's 2019-20 #BestColleges List. (n.d.). Retrieved from https://money.com/best-colleges/profile/university-of-california-irvine/

CHAPTER 5

"I Wish Someone Had Told Me It Was Going to Be Like This": Lessons Learned as a PhD Student

Marisa V. Cervantes

I will never forget the day I received my acceptance to graduate school. I was at work when my phone buzzed notifying me of a new email. With my heart racing, I clicked on the message and shut my eyes preparing for a rejection. When I opened my eyes and saw "Congratulations!," I couldn't breathe. *Did I just get into a PhD program??* I hadn't gotten to the point of imagining this moment because in all honesty, I didn't want to get my hopes up for something I wasn't even sure would happen.

That evening, I walked into my house to find my mom sitting on the couch. Right away she knew something was wrong. Before she could ask, I handed her my phone with the email opened on the screen. With tears streaming down my cheeks and a knot in my throat, I said, "Mom, they actually want me." We hugged and cried for what seemed like an eternity. Now that my mom knew, it was real.

A few months later, I packed up and moved to this tiny town with nothing but white people with the hopes of following my dreams. I knew the pursuit of a doctoral degree would be a rough journey that would challenge me intellectually and push me beyond anything I had experienced before in my educational career. However, I was not prepared for the additional difficulties that have come with it. I quickly realized that my academic accomplishments, research experience, and passion to teach were not enough to help me combat the persistent imposter syndrome through each stage of the doctoral journey. More than that, I was not prepared for the challenges that would come as a result of my intersecting identities.

As a fifth year in my program, I've completed my coursework, earned a Master's degree, became a doctoral candidate embarking on my dissertation research, and am an instructor. Yet after all of this time I'm still asking myself the same question: *why didn't anyone tell me it was going to be this hard?*

∙ ∙ ∙

Soon after I'd been invited to write this essay is when news of the college admissions scandal broke. You know, the one with Aunt Becky and the other rich white folks who paid to have their kids admitted to college. Of course, it was no surprise that this was happening and that people at various stages of the education system were complicit in it. Yet, despite my personal experience and knowledge of social inequality, I had to take time to process it.

After years of feeling like I didn't belong in my schools and in my classes, feeling like I wasn't smart enough and didn't know enough and fearing that one day someone was going to call me out on my incompetence, I realized just how *backwards* this all was. *They are the imposters, not us*. Not the first-generation students of color from working-class families who have had to overcome things that the privileged cannot even imagine.

I thought of the cold November night during my first semester of grad school when I texted my mentor from my undergrad years in tears because I had to lead discussion for my Theory Seminar the next day. All semester I struggled in that class; I agonized over it every week because no matter how many times I read and re-read, I always felt stupid like I couldn't keep up with my classmates. That night, I knew in my heart that my professor, classmates, and soon the entire department would find out that I wasn't meant to be here. After wallowing for a few hours, I decided that if I was going to fail, at least it would be after I gave it my best effort, so I worked all night and contacted my professor, letting her know that I had a really hard time with the material but hoped I'd covered the right topics.

The presentation went better than expected – and by that, I mean I didn't get chewed out in class, I didn't run out of there crying, and I didn't completely fail the assignment. At that point, I didn't care about the grade I'd end up with; I was just relieved that it was over.

•••

I'm ashamed to say that I've always followed the rules and did what I was told in school. As a first-gen student, I was scared that if I didn't do it the way I was supposed to, I'd fail. It wasn't until I got to grad school that I really started to understand how I've been adhering to white, heteronormative, patriarchal standards in these institutions. As an undergrad I was fortunate to find a mentor who understood me, encouraged me, and pushed me like no one ever had before. When my work wasn't good enough, she made me do it again. When I was struggling to focus on my schoolwork, she set me straight. When I needed comforting, she was there for me in ways that my family couldn't be. As a first-gen herself, she guided me through college and has continued to be there for me in grad school.

Because I haven't had the same type of mentorship in my graduate program, it's forced me to be my own advocate, which has been a challenge in itself. I've wanted to quit more times than I can count. The repeated microaggressions and unequal treatment that I experienced forced me to make some changes. Little by little, my confidence has grown, and I've been able to speak up, ask for help, and let my professors know what I need.

The most significant way that I've done this is through changing advisors halfway through my third year while I was doing my comprehensive exams. I worked really hard on the first component of the exam, had my advisor review my work, received positive feedback from her, and felt confident in what I submitted. When I received the news that I hadn't passed because I'd failed to clearly address my dissertation plans, I was furious. My advisor had reviewed my work, after all. After taking a few days to calm down, I met with another professor to ask if she would be my primary advisor because I didn't trust the other one to get me through the next phase of the exams, and definitely not through the dissertation. In my eyes, this situation was completely her fault. It's not like I was her first student, nor was it the first time she'd reviewed these exams. It was *my* first time, however, and I'd sent multiple drafts for her to look over. I asked for help, addressed the few comments she gave me and asked for help again. When my advisor tells me "this looks great!" how do I accept that I've failed?

I don't.

Because *I* didn't fail. She failed me.

Although the professor agreed to be my new advisor, I still had to meet with the other one and let her know that I was switching. I'd wrestled with the idea of changing advisors for about a year because I knew I was not receiving the mentorship that I deserved. I found myself coming up with reasons not to switch despite multiple issues that had occurred and overall frustrations with the lack of support I was receiving. This incident, however, was the last straw.

I was nervous. Like any grad student can tell you, the power dynamics are real! There is always a fear of retaliation when it comes to switching advisors or addressing issues with a professor. I was worried about the potential consequences; would she still be willing to work with me? What about the work we already had in progress? Will this impact me outside of the department? With the support of my new advisor and encouragement from my small circle, I knew this was what I needed, both for my own peace of mind and success in the program.

The day had come to meet and inform her that she would no longer be my advisor. As I sat in her office listening to her apologize and shed tears over the mistake that she made, I couldn't help but get mad all over again. I'd done the work to process my emotions and reaffirm to myself that this wasn't my fault and that things would work out. The re-write process wouldn't be hard; I could get it done in no time. But now, sitting in her office, I had to do the emotional labor while she cried for herself at her failure as a mentor. Not once did I say "it's okay" when she apologized, because it's not okay that marginalized students like me, a first-generation woman of color, have to comfort a white woman who has been in academia for over a decade over a mistake that does not impact her career.

I have told my committee members multiple times that I'm a first-generation college student, and I do not know what I don't know. These words leave a bittersweet taste in my mouth. On one hand, I feel embarrassed to have to admit that I need help or that I don't know many things that my peers seem to know. On the other hand, I know that it's for everyone's benefit. Them knowing that I'm a first-gen student and that my lack of knowledge is something they need to help me with is going to make them better mentors to future first-gen students who enter this program. And it's going to not only help me obtain my degree, but I'll also become a better mentor. The undergrad first-gen students that I've worked with over these past four years have shown me that I am making a difference. As hard as it is, by advocating for myself, I'm advocating for others. And that's what I came here to do.

•••

I grew up in a town that was once the murder capital of the nation. My community was riddled by gangs, drugs, and all-around violence. I vividly remember the first time I saw a man beating on a woman in public. It was a cold, cloudy morning and my mom was dropping off my brother and me at my *tia's* house before she would drive us to school. We pulled up to the house and were about to exit the car when we saw a car pulling out of the driveway two houses down. A man came running out, and in the middle of the street he punched through the driver side window, breaking the glass, and kept punching at the woman. My mom pulled the door shut so that we couldn't get out and told us to get down. Ducking down was nothing new. We knew that when we heard gunshots we needed to get down on the ground below the windows. But this was something I hadn't seen before. All day long, I replayed that scene in my mind. When my teacher told me multiple times to pay attention, I lifted my head so she'd think I was listening. But all I could hear was the woman screaming and the man's voice saying he was going to kill her. My teacher had no idea what my morning was like and there was no way I was going to tell her I'd just witnessed someone being beaten in the street. The white people at school were too scared to even go to my hood, why would I share something like this with them? Since that day in the first grade, every time I've passed by that house, I've wondered what ever happened to that woman.

As a single mother, my mom relied on the help of our family to care for us. Regardless of all that my family has suffered throughout the years, from absent fathers and domestic violence to alcoholism and drug abuse, shootings, incarcerations and death, the one thing that always stayed with me is that it takes a village to get through it and that when one of us succeeds, we all do.

I learned quickly that people like me weren't supposed to "make it." When I graduated high school with honors and without a pregnancy, we had succeeded. When I went to college and graduated with honors, that was a victory for my entire family. I had a caravan of thirty-plus people make a six-hour road trip to be there for my big day. When I crossed that stage, it was as if they'd all crossed it with me. And when I become the first person to earn a PhD ... well, I can't put into words what that will mean.

What I do know, however, is that no matter how far I get in this life and in my career, I will never forget where I came from or what my village has given me. My community taught me that even in the worst circumstances, we will survive. My chance at an education taught me that we shouldn't just be surviving, but we should be thriving (hooks, 1993). By blending these two parts of my life, I know that I have a responsibility to teach others about the oppressive systems that target our communities so that we can change them.

At the same time, I've learned that this responsibility that I've taken on is not going to be accepted by everyone. And as difficult as it's been for me, I've learned that when I speak out and try to show others in my family and in my community how this country's systems work to keep the poor poor and the non-white inferior, it can be taken as a personal attack. I've lost relationships with family members because I speak out against white supremacy, anti-Blackness (especially in the Latinx community), machismo, and for calling out the façade of the meritocracy of this country.

My outspokenness is considered rude to some; others say that I think I'm better than them because I went to college. While these comments hurt at first, I've gotten to a place where I understand that I'm no longer the same person I was before, and I view this as a good thing. Why would I want to sit still, ignorant and complicit to the systems and ways of thinking that have made it so that people like me are considered the "lucky ones" while in the same conversation, we lament about the misfortune that is my cousin. Someone who is two years older than me, who grew up in the same community as me and with whom I spent almost every day together as kids. When he dropped out of his freshman year at the local public university because he couldn't afford tuition, he went down a different path and is now serving a 60-year prison sentence.

I refuse to credit this as solely due to luck or misfortune. This discrepancy is proof that this country has done everything in its power to keep Black and Brown people wrapped up in the system rather than in any other institution. I refuse to stay quiet and allow family members to spew their victim-blaming rhetoric and racist comments, to listen to them glorify white people and tell me that I owe my life to white people because without them I wouldn't have my education or my degrees. "No," I say, "I have my degrees *in spite of them.*" Because at every stage of my education, I've had to bite my tongue when they tell me how surprised they are that I've made it this far. So now that I have the chance to do the teaching, I'm committed to teaching the truth, no matter how uncomfortable it makes people feel.

•••

The lessons I've learned since being in my doctoral program transcend the objectives of each seminar, research project, or assistantship. As I begin my dissertation, all I can think about is how much I've had to fight just to get to this point. This experience has consistently shown me that academia wasn't made for us. I came in thinking that this process and the degree I'll eventually obtain would allow me to do the work I aspired to do. I quickly learned that isn't the case. I've gotten pushback for just about every change I've tried to make, whether in choosing different books for the classes that I teach or trying to develop a mentorship program for underrepresented students in my department. I've learned that when one of us makes it into these spaces, we're vilified and made to feel as though we have to change who we are in order to fit in or give up on trying to make change because it's just going to cause more damage.

Despite having attended predominantly white schools my entire life and even living in Europe for a semester, coming to this place for grad school was the biggest culture shock of my life. Since living in this tiny town, I've realized how much my hometown gave me. The homesickness I felt in college was nothing compared to the emptiness and loneliness I've experienced here. Riding the busses, being in my department, and living in this town, I am often the only brown face in a sea of white.

As one of the few people of color in my department, the constant feelings of isolation, (in)visibility, and marginalization have made navigating graduate school a complex and vicious process. Despite feeling like I'm walking on eggshells every time I step foot into these toxic spaces, this experience has shown me over and over that like my ancestors, I am resilient. At the end of the day, I, a first-generation Latina from the hood, deserve to be here just as much as anyone else and no one can take that from me.

Acknowledgements

To my mom, who has been by my side every step of the way; to the mujeres who raised me; to my resilient community; and to LT, who has guided me in this journey. Thank you.

Reference

hooks, b. (1993). *Sisters of the yam: Black women and self-recovery.* South End Press.

CHAPTER 6

Black and in Grad School: Demystifying the Intersections of Race and Gender in Higher Education

LaToya W. Brown

My college days in undergrad were a pleasant memory of self-discovery, activism, and community. My alma mater, a Historically Black College and University (HBCU), North Carolina Agricultural and Technical State University, was, for me, the Mecca. It was the place where I was both intellectually and culturally stimulated. As a first generation, Black female college student, NC A&T gave me the strength and guidance I needed that I have continued to draw from throughout my life. As I navigated through undergrad, I found professors that were supportive, those that listened, and those that wanted to see me succeed. I found my identity in syllabi and readings that celebrated the Black experience, while engaging classroom discussions painted a picture of how the outside world viewed my community. Though readings by James Baldwin, Alice Walker, Richard Wright, and Zora Neale Hurston, to name a few, reminded me of the struggles Black people face in America, they also left me feeling empowered, resilient and determined to navigate the complex social world. A&T somewhat sheltered me from the demons of the outside world – systematic inequality, criminalization, racism, etc. – while providing a space where I felt liberated. Through shared experiences, I developed some of my most solid bonds with other students and faculty members that I value today. Unfortunately, what A&T did not prepare me for was how to navigate the haunting intersections of race and gender in graduate school.

My transition to a predominantly white institution (PWI) to pursue a PhD, since obtaining my bachelor's and master's degrees at NC A&T SU, has been one of trials and triumphs. I, like many other Black students, struggle with staying the course and graduating, and I think this is due to a lack of an ethic of care that is almost non-existent in these graduate programs. Simply put, the experience in my own graduate program has, at times, lacked initiatives to support and nurture marginalized students throughout their process. This includes first generation college students. At A&T, I had professors who nurtured me, checked in with me regularly, and were easier to connect to because they looked like me and shared some of my same experiences. Since attending a PWI, I have, at times, felt the exact opposite. The support that was once readily available is now harder to come by. While many advisors provide some support, Black students need critical communities that help them navigate the hidden curriculum, or the unwritten rules, that are vital to their success. The same ready-made community of Black excellence and support that I quickly found at A&T was not as easy to find at the PWI where I enrolled. Also, the demographics of the classroom shifted, as I again was outnumbered by my white colleagues. In classes where my culture was previously highlighted and celebrated, I now found myself struggling to find representation of myself on course syllabi and readings. Coming from an HBCU where I had access to a number of support, peers and Black female faculty members, I walked the halls to find one Black faculty member, a female, who was bombarded with students of color begging for advisement, encouragement, and nurture. I, too, needed her to be my spirit-guide just as I needed my other Black professors who willingly took on this role at my previous HBCU. Having this lack of representation certainly conveyed the haunting reality of being devalued and unwelcomed in academia.

For many Black students, there is a constant wrestle between feeling validated, having support, and having spaces where we can be authentic. This, coupled with being a first generation student, produces even greater challenges. I have often felt a great deal of pressure to succeed; the fear of failure and the imposter syndrome – the perception of not being qualified – often haunts me. This has particularly affected me as a Black woman and often left me feeling inadequate, not smart enough, and not cut out for grad school. Because of this, in graduate classes, I've often felt myself holding back during classroom discussions, whereas in undergrad, I would've felt more comfortable and confident. In addition, I have had to absorb a good amount of debt, as my family is not wealthy enough to pay for my education. This haunts me as a woman of color because it creates an innate fear of not being able to provide for my family, and it creates a huge amount of pressure to secure a good paying job after graduating. As a first-generation college student, I already feel the burden of responsibility to myself, my family and my community; I feel like my accomplishment in earning a PhD is so much greater than me.

Though I have had to face these challenges, there are several things that have helped me to survive. Those things are: establishing my own support network, being ok with failure, advocating for myself, and making time for self-care. One of the most important things for me was to find my critical community. In my graduate courses, it seemed as if the Black students gravitated to one another. It was almost as if there was an unspoken cry for help amongst each of us. Fortunately, we exchanged numbers, emails, and decided to form a summer reading group with the lone Black female professor as our guide. We began by reading texts by Black feminist authors like Patricia Hill Collins and bell hooks to name a few. Our conversations focused on celebrating Black womanhood, navigating white spaces, building community with one another and just simply checking in and reminding each other we were not alone. Overtime, this eventually turned into a support group, that we refer to as "The Crew," where we interact with each other and share similar experiences. We celebrate each other's successes, both in and outside of the university, and we uplift each other in times of need, failure, and pure exhaustion.

As a first-generation college student, there's no one in my family that I can look to for advice because no one has gone before me. In my own experience, graduate school seems like a cycle of demystifying the pipeline to the PhD, while trying to sustain my mental health along the way. From choosing an advisor, dissertation committee, and publishing opportunities, everything seems like some big secret I'm not privy to know. What I have found most helpful in terms of cracking this code is connecting back to The Crew because we share opportunities with one another and advise each another on how to advocate for ourselves. What I have come to realize is graduate school is a game of survival of the fittest, and as a Black female student in graduate school at a PWI, having to play this game is exhausting. As previously stated, being faced with a lack of role models who share the same cultural experiences and values as I do has often left me feeling isolated and further confirms the narrative that Black women are devalued in academia. Thus, the road to the PhD is a balance between thriving and surviving, while being forced to navigate multiple identities and the pressures of being Black.

Traditional pedagogy – racist, sexist, classist, etc. – in higher education has silenced many students of color, as Black intellectuals have been devalued in the American education system. Student minds are policed by a system that teaches them to not question, engage, or challenge. As a Black female educator that teaches primarily Black students and pre-service teachers, helping students find their voice in a system that has silenced them since their first encounter is critical. Some of the topics we dissect are racist ideology, patriarchy, and how American systems reproduce inequalities and inequities. In this regard, I encourage my students to think of themselves as strong people with important things to contribute, and then challenge them to perform at a higher level rather than just doing enough to get by or get a certain grade. As a Black female educator, it is my duty to disrupt the hegemonic, colonized methods for educating students. Instead, I seek to enact a pedagogy that reflects wholeness, spirituality, and inclusiveness, which will ignite passion and activism in my students. Bringing about transformation and empowerment with the students I encounter is a main goal of mine. In my classes, building community is important. I seek to co-create, with my students, spaces where we can trust and be vulnerable with one another. We talk about how we can learn from our individual stories and experiences, and we share our personal connections to course material. Black students often struggle in education because, as I found, our knowledge, culture and experiences are often silenced, while those of the dominant group are imposed. It becomes critical to get students to value themselves and their intellectual ability. I am responsible for creating an environment where my students feel both empowered and liberated. Liberatory education will not only help Black students regain their voice. It will also help them reclaim their agency. Through liberatory education, students can recognize the politics of education and the struggle for freedom and justice. It is a vehicle for change, it raises consciousness, and it validates the experiences of marginalized groups. It is important to me as an educator to bridge the cultural experiences of my students with that of the dominant culture so students learn how to coexist, recognize and dismantle hegemonic, oppressive ideology.

What I have learned to accept is grad school will always be a battlefield for students of color. We are battling against white dominated spaces where our opinions aren't valued, we often must validate our research, and we are often stripped of our voices. Thus, advocating for more faculty members of color and finding and building critical communities are essential to the success of Black academics. Yes, there may be times when our views won't be understood, but it's up to us to be respected, and the one thing that is true about us is we are resilient and we will continue to rise.

CHAPTER 7

Locating Struggles with Sociology and Surviving with Mindfulness

Matt Reid

When I attended the afternoon orientation at my community college as an eighteen-year-old, I had virtually no understanding of higher education. As a first-generation college student, I did not know what a credit hour was, I had no idea what I wanted to study, and I was the only one in the orientation group who had not yet completed my FASFA paperwork. Yet I was an exceptional student in high school and graduated within the top 20% of my class, earning a spot in a new state program that would cover the tuition for two years at a community college and another two years at any state school. This financial assistance enabled me to attend college without having to worry much about debt, and in some small way, shifted my career focus from one of financial gain to one of personal fulfillment. As I approach my thirties, I am nearing the completion of my PhD in Sociology with hopes of becoming a (tenure-track) college professor. Maybe it was sheer coincidence, but the first physical class I attended as a college freshman was Sociology 101. It was a class that spoke to me as both a gay man and as someone from a working-class family.

My conservative high school taught comprehensive sexual education but conveniently excluded anything about sexual orientation or sexuality. The few times I recall homosexuality being discussed were in a psychology class in the contexts of sexual perversions and mental illness. There were also only a handful of openly gay people at my high school of over a thousand students. These individuals were often targeted with vicious teasing under the tacit approval of the school staff. I realized that I wasn't as brave as these visibly queer people and knew coming out then would not have been a wise choice.

Sociology provides us with the conceptual tools to interrogate our imperfect world (Schwalbe, 1998/2018, 2020). It is a discipline that appeals to those who have experienced injustices stemming from classism, racism, sexism, heterosexism, and all other social systems which privilege one group at the oppression of others. By making these inequalities visible through critical discourse, sociology enabled me to better understand my social location and everyday frustrations. Since I am socially privileged in the areas of race and gender, my personal worries have primarily focused on class mobility and heteronormative assumptions. For over a decade I have tried explaining this to my parents in various ways. They still have no clue what I study or do for a living.

Yet sociology has allowed me to enrich my understanding of my place in the social world. For example, I can locate the source of my marginalization as a gay person within our society's privileging of heterosexual lifestyles. I can also appreciate how my working-class upbringing has affected my preoccupation with financial security. Unlike many college students who dream of large paychecks and early retirement, I desire job security and my definition of "making it" is merely being debt-free. I don't aspire to a McMansion or luxury vehicle, but rather the freedom from compounding interest on student loans and credit cards.

Sociology not only illuminates personal situations, but it also critiques oppressive entities. Sometimes these are obvious (e.g., heteronormativity and capitalism), but privileging can also manifest in subtler ways as it does in higher education. For example, even though you are expected to attend academic conferences, it is a privilege to attend these as many institutions offer little or no funding for conference travel (Kelsky, 2015). I am fortunate that my R2 university was able to offset conferences costs associated with regional conferences, but it was also frustrating that a significant out-of-pocket expense would be incurred at national conferences held in expensive cities. It is also a privilege to be able to afford graduate school without working one or more jobs outside of the academy. Scarce and competitive graduate assistantships help greatly here, but even the $12,000 per year I received as a master's student was not enough to live on. The time I spent researching and applying for government aid, working odd jobs, and participating in market research studies is ultimately time I could have used to complete my degree more expeditiously.

The structure of academia privileges those who are already financially secure and/or can receive material support from others. This places first-generation students at a disadvantage since they are more likely to come from working-class families. While a college education is not a guarantee of a middle-class lifestyle, education and wealth are tightly intertwined. While I was an undergraduate, both of my parents lost their long-held positions in the service sector, and neither was able to find another job anywhere near as decent as their last. They didn't have any savings, they ended up losing their little house, and they are now each on disability related to medical conditions that intensified after their terminations. Needless to say, I cannot rely on them for material support, and I will inherit only debt whenever they pass.

Working in academia can also be a weird experience for first-gen, working-class individuals. As a graduate student, most of my waking hours were dedicated to academic endeavors like course work and research, as well as the assistance given to other professors, my department, my university, and my discipline. However, none of this immediately benefited my financial wellbeing as there were no paths to promotion or pay increases available to graduate assistants like myself. Meanwhile, I have seen most of my non-academic friends rewarded with various promotions, start their retirement savings, put a down payment on a house, and achieve various other milestones of adulthood regardless of their education level. While I wouldn't say I am jealous of their success, I envy the appearance of stability they have found in their lives. I doubt they spend much of their time worrying if they'll be able to afford to eat in the summer since they don't need to rely on semesterly contracts or annual funding decisions. For the past several years, my summers have been marked by food insecurity and biweekly trips to plasma donation centers (and yes, I lie on the same-sex activity question).

Another example of subtle privileging can be in how academia may impact one's relationship with parents. As I spend the majority of my time doing some sort of academic work, I find it increasingly tiresome to explain the details to my parents. They typically do not remember what I say about degree requirements, levels of academic employment, or anything related to working in a college environment. This is not their fault and may be attributable to an unequal opportunity structure that impeded their enrollment in the academy as high school graduates from working-class families. In other words, they never had the privilege of participating in an academic institution or working towards a degree, and this disadvantage impacts family dynamics if/when someone achieves a post-graduate education. Whenever I attempt to communicate my struggles to them, they are not able to respond with anything other than "you can do it" or some other vague encouragement. Moreover, I've generally grown tired of repeating to them the dissertation process time and time again, and why I am still poor even though I technically work at a university. They do not know the regimentation within the academy and how much the pay scale diverges between part-time, full-time, and tenure-track positions. I have finally come to accept that I cannot make them knowledgeable about my career path at this point in their lives.

My point here is to say that my growth as a scholar has resulted in a great divide between the experiences of my parents and myself. Another part of that divide is that I am a (radical) gay man with no desire to live a heteronormative life marked by marriage and children. I know marriage equality has been a significant achievement for the gay rights movement, but it is not something I have ever aspired to. Though I feel somewhat alienated from my family, I do not feel totally at home within the academic community either. Not only am I at the bottom of the academic ladder as a graduate student and more recently as a contingent faculty member, but most of my colleagues and superiors are straight, financially stable, and/or come from college-educated families. Furthermore, my guiding philosophy is best captured in the words of John Waters (2017): "Go out in the world and fuck it up beautifully" (p. 59). This does not align with polite models of social change favored by academic administrators or those who believe social science should be apolitical.

Truth be told, I never felt an imposter because I have yet to feel as if I am a complete member of the academy. Every position I have held so far has been temporary, and I always felt my role was distinct from faculty and other permanent academics. Another way of saying this is that I never felt like an imposter because I have always felt like a *known* outsider or someone conspicuously not part of the core community. Some of this could be my penchant for nonconformity, but I believe my outsider status is primarily a product of structural stipulations. For example, graduate students work hard with hopes of exiting the role as quickly as possible. It is certainly not a role to relish, and reminders of subservience abound in personal interactions, official communications, and institutional resources like support services and benefit packages. Likewise, when I took a full-time visiting faculty position at a nearby state college, the limit of three renewals on my yearly contract clearly sent the message to not get cozy. It would be another thing if a path for advancement was built into the position, but no matter the quality of my work, I would once again become an adjunct after three years. Budget cuts and constraints on new faculty lines also mean a permanent position is unlikely to become available.

While I do not think I have experienced imposter syndrome, my mental health was far from optimal at the start of my PhD program. My break down in June 2015 was the cumulation of years of nonstop and redundant course work, inadequate access to mental health care, and a lack of mentoring regarding comprehensive examinations. It was not a sudden thing either, as the entire preceding semester was a struggle where my abilities to read and write floundered. In retrospect, my deterioration was visibly obvious, but I could not visit campus mental health resources more than I already was. Their staff was stretched thin and appointments were scarce, and the faculty members I was working with did not seem to notice. I remember getting 15 pages written by the end of the five-day exam time, roughly 45 short of the expectation. I knew it was terrible, and I unsurprisingly failed that significant milestone in my doctoral studies. The next year would be challenging as well, and I fell behind on a handful of independent studies in my degree program. I felt lost and abandoned, especially as I had fully devoted the last several years of my life to graduate school. The faculty I had previously worked with seemed to look upon me as a problematic case, as someone best dealt with through cold but efficient bureaucratic processes, and I received the "unacceptable progress" letter following that year's annual review. My funding was gone, I had to take on more classes as an adjunct for a fraction of the pay, and I still had several incompletes to rectify.

Fortunately, soon after I failed my comprehensive exam, I enrolled in a graduate-level course on mindfulness meditation. My shallow thinking was that this would be an easy elective, but the class fundamentally changed my life and approach to academia. Mindfulness practices are those that orient our attention toward the present moment. Focusing on the breath, for example, helps prevent our minds from ruminating on the past or imagining unlikely future scenarios. More simply stated, mindfulness helps us live in the moment rather than in our disappointing pasts or anxiety-provoking futures (Kabat-Zinn, 1994). Formal practices like meditation gradually enabled me to recognize and disrupt non-present thinking in my daily life.

My foray into mindfulness practices came at a low point in my life, and it took me about a year to recover my academic spirit. It also allowed me to come to peace with my place in the academy and larger social structure. I am a first-generation graduate student who realizes much can be fixed within the academy, but I am not yet in a position where I can effectively transform the structure. I can let elitism, classism, and heterosexism consume my thought processes, but this will only impede my ability to rise out of the tenuous professional position of a graduate student. While working in the discipline of sociology necessitates constant consideration of these social forces, there is a big difference between attention *given to* and attention *dominated by* inequality.

It may sound like heresy for a sociologist to say this, but since it is not within my power to single-handedly change the status quo, I try not to let oppressions overwhelm my thoughts. I still go to the plasma donation center and I regularly encounter homophobes, but when I am not directly dealing with these things, I do not want to think about class or sexuality privilege. Compared to those whose attention to inequality is merely intellectual, poverty and heterosexism place constraints on my daily life. They are both physically and socially inescapable, so the only immediate respite available to me is psychological. I am also aware that my gender and race privilege make this temporary peace of mind more readily achievable. However, knowing this affirms my commitment to fighting for equality.

Some people critique mindfulness as egotistical and contrary to the goals of social justice. I find this to be a misdirected argument because mindful acceptance does not tell you to give up on social change. It simply makes one realize that your frustrations and anxieties result from situations beyond your control and that the only things you can control in the present moment are your thinking and actions. You can let injustices overwhelm your thoughts, but this might hamper your abilities to more effectively confront these issues later. For example, I can do more to transform graduate education for first-generation students as a professor than I could as a graduate student. But as a graduate student, I often found myself ruminating on the displeasure of my situation which distracted me from moving ahead. Furthermore, I learned that I could still find satisfaction while living with a status that I could not immediately change.

While I can rage against the alienation of graduate studies, I can make more of a positive difference elsewhere. Since many of my students are also first-generation, I use a lot of personal experiences as examples in class, particularly those which relate to my working-class upbringing and my ongoing struggle for financial stability. My goal in doing this is to educate while illustrating survival strategies and the importance of the cultural capital gained from a college education. I routinely share with my classes practical insights like strategies for living independently, navigating bureaucracies, and maintaining good mental health. Yet I also share with them how education results in more opportunities and a richer understanding of social life. By sharing my struggles and failures, and how I have overcome these obstacles, I hope to dispel the mentality of "I'm just not good enough" while shifting their attention to structural rather than individual faults. I also come out to my students on the first day of class, and I know my visibility has been an inspiration to many queer students. Overall, I have fun doing these things, and it enlivens my spirit when I see it make a difference.

When I began teaching full-time several years ago, I gradually realized that my degree program had become less central in my life. Not that I had given up or slacked off, just the opposite, in fact. As I distanced myself from my grad department, my professors, and my peers, I felt liberated from the nonsense associated with grad life. There was less status boasting and no more disempowering "advice" about the decline of academia. Public education at all levels is under attack, but sometimes the expressed frustrations of my superiors would only come across as contemptuous. Dissatisfaction with one's job was the norm in my working-class upbringing, but the expectation was to quietly keep pushing on. I would recommend faculty be conscious of the message grumbling sends to aspiring professors. It's one thing to relay factual information about poor campus governance, but please do so without the implication that "you'll never land a job in the field."

As of writing this essay, I am completing the first draft of my dissertation and applying for tenure-track positions. I do not think I would be at this point if I had not cleansed my mind of distracting frustrations or found a trusted advisor with an understanding of mental health. My doctoral work has taken nearly six years, but since there is nothing I can do to alter the past, I focus my mind on things that bring me joy. I know the job market for sociology PhDs had deteriorated, but I'm still sending out applications and putting faith in my history of overcoming obstacles. I *cannot* control what positions become available or how hiring committees rank my application relative to others. I *can* control how I use my time, and I choose to be free of worry and to engage my students with mutually beneficial enthusiasm.

References

Kabat-Zinn, J. (1994). *Wherever you go, there you are: Mindfulness meditation in everyday life.* Hyperion.

Kelsky, K. (2015). *The professor is in: The essential guide to turning your Ph.D. into a job.* Three Rivers Press.

Schwalbe, M. (2018). *The sociologically examined life: Pieces of conversation.* Oxford University Press. (Original work published 1998)

Schwalbe, M. (2020). *Making a difference: Using sociology to create a better world.* Oxford University Press.

Waters, J. (2017). *Make trouble.* Algonquin Books.

CHAPTER 8

From the Mekong and Delaware River to the Merrimack River: The Unintentional Road to the Doctorate

Phitsamay Sychitkokhong Uy and Francine Rudd Coston

This chapter starts with two narratives, one of Phitsamay, a Lao refugee first-generation faculty member, followed by Francine, an African American first-generation doctoral student from Philadelphia. Phitsamay first met Francine in her role as graduate coordinator of the doctoral program in Leadership in Schooling and eventually became her dissertation chair. Over the years they have gotten to know each other's personal and professional lives. This chapter also illuminates the similarities in their experiences on their unintentional road to the academy. They conclude with recommendations for colleges and universities to consider in supporting their first-generation doctoral students.

Phitsamay – Secretly Hiding in Plain Sight

Laos was the most heavily bombed country per capita in history. From 1964 to 1973, the US dropped more than two million tons of ordnance on Laos during 580,000 bombing missions – equal to a planeload of bombs every 8 minutes, 24-hours a day, for 9 years. The bombings destroyed many villages causing hundreds of thousands of Lao civilians to seek refuge in neighboring countries and abroad. My family was one of those families seeking refuge first in a Thai refugee camp and eventually in the United States.

Growing up in a Lao refugee family, I never heard of a dissertation or anyone who had earned a doctorate. In fact, my family never talked about college; my mother was happy that her girls got to go to high school since she never was given that chance. While we struggled economically like other poor families, our struggles were marked by post-traumatic stress disorder (PTSD); our trauma made us fearful of government officials who wanted to collect data on families since this was how the Lao government rounded up any American sympathizers and put people into "re-education" camps. We also lived in a culture of silence. My parents never talked about the bombings nor of their fear of political persecution. We were taught to obey the rules and fly under the radar so as not to be detected.

I attribute my academic success to the social network (Coleman, 1988) that my parents built for the family. Because my refugee parents lacked familiarity with US school systems, they did not understand the roles each school staff played nor the expectations for their involvement. Their main responsibility as parents was to provide a safe haven from the bombs, food in our bellies and clothes for our bodies. Their lack of English proficiency prevented them from helping with homework and giving any other concrete advice for navigating the US school system. All that information came from our social network of neighbors, teachers, and friends' family members. It was because of those people that I managed to graduate high school, earn a bachelor's degree, and eventually pursue a doctorate.

The doctorate degree was an accident. In fact, I am an accidental academic (Rose, David, & Woodward, 1998). I credit my roommate for this accomplishment because I would not have applied without her concrete advice and suggestions. In 1998, I attended an education conference where I learned about the high dropout rate of our Southeast Asians students. I asked people at the conference, what is happening in the schools and communities to produce such a high dropout rate? No one had a response for me. That is when my Chinese-American friend Carolyn told me, "That is what a dissertation is for. When you have a burning question that only you can answer." My response to her was, "I am only an elementary school teacher. What do I know about conducting research, let alone writing a dissertation?"

With the help of my friends, I worked through those doubts and applied for doctoral study. In fact, it was through Carolyn's guidance and her belief in me that I even considered applying to Harvard – I always thought Harvard was for those smart people not a Lao refugee like me. She had gotten accepted into the new academic program called Communities and School which was (at the time) led by Pedro Noguera. Carolyn advised me to make an appointment with Pedro so he could meet me and then advocate for my application. Not knowing how I would finance my doctorate, I deliberately wrote on my application that I would only enroll in a program that would provide me with financial funding and support. Luckily for me Pedro advocated for me to attend and receive the coveted Harvard Presidential Fellowship which provided three years of funding.

At the end of the third year, I remember crying on the side steps of Gutman Library because I did not know how I was going to pay for rent that month. Like other first-generation students, I did not map out in entirety how I was going to fund the doctorate degree. The only thing I planned out was the organization of two bags: one full of my books and another filled with food to appease my hunger throughout the day. This habit was a residual impact of being malnourished for two years in the refugee camp. I now always keep food and drinks in my office to offer to my students and colleagues in case any of them are ever hungry. It took me nine years to finish my doctoral studies because I went back to work at the start of my fourth year when the funding ran out.

Francine – Wearing the Mask That Grins and Lies

Paul Laurence Dunbar, the African American author of the poem, "We Wear the Mask," was among the first generation born of freed Black slaves. Even with freedom and validation as a poet, he still expressed the need to wear the mask. This is my mask, too.

I had a childhood friend whose mother was an elementary school teacher. She was the only person, male or female, that had a college degree on our block. So, education was very important in that family. All of the children were expected to go to college. I admired that about my friend's family, even envied it. She inspired me as well. I was proud to be an honor roll student throughout my K-12 years in the Philadelphia school district. However in college, when I did not achieve honors in my first semester, nor my second, third, or fourth semester, I began to wonder if I, an African American female, the youngest of eleven siblings, was smart enough for the University of Delaware. I felt so out of place. I felt like I didn't belong there. The language was different (e.g., syllabus, bursar, academic advisor, registrar, etc.). I wondered, "What are they talking about, and why am I the only one who doesn't have a clue?" My college friends, roommates, and classmates all had family and friends who had attended college and knew the language and how to navigate the college system. I felt like I was always a few steps behind or a little late, and had to work twice as hard just to stay afloat. I was doing badly, emotionally and academically. Perhaps my high school counselor had made a big mistake by encouraging me to attend college? Am I wearing a mask and deceiving others into believing that I was college material?

Attending a predominantly white institution meant that there sometimes were racial tensions on campus but as an undergraduate student I did not experience them because I often went home for the weekends. Since I was constantly homesick, I decided to tell my family that I was leaving school at the end of my second semester. I also felt like I was wasting my time and everyone's money. But the afternoon before heading back to campus, I overheard my mother on the telephone speaking to a good friend of hers. "My baby is so smart," she said, "and will be the first one to get a college degree. I am so proud of her. When she graduates, we are bringing the entire family to graduation." When I heard that, there was no way I was going to let my family down. I went back that weekend, determined to graduate. It took me four and a half years to receive my Bachelor's degree and I even made the Dean's list a few times.

It had been 10 years since my family and I moved from the south to New England In 2011, we came kicking and screaming, much to my husband's dismay. His new job required us to relocate. Because the children were still so young, I took the opportunity to stay at home and not rush back into a job. This allowed me to explore other career aspirations while getting settled into a new area. Then with two degrees in hand, I began the job search. After several months with no leads, I came across a position at the local university. It was a coordinator position for a grant-funded program that provided academic support and financial resources for underrepresented students. I immediately thought about my high school counselor and the support she provided to me. I was offered the position and instantly knew I had found the perfect job. The persistence and resilience I saw in the students often reminded me of myself. As a first-generation college student, I understood their challenges. I made it my mission to ensure they would receive the guidance through academic advising, support with tutoring services, and resources that provided stipends for textbooks and school supplies needed to be able to succeed.

As I grew in my position and aspired to develop my knowledge and skills, I once again started to feel the dreadful feeling of being left behind. Working in higher education and attending college are two different experiences. Like before, the language used by my coworkers (i.e., retention, attrition, student involvement and engagement) left me feeling out of place. I began thinking about returning to school to get another degree but this time in the field of education. Since my previous degrees were not in education, I felt that getting a firm foundation rooted in education, specifically higher education, would allow me to better support the students I work with. I thought to myself, "Where do I start? How do I do it? Where was that guidance counselor when I needed her?" During my time at the university, I had the chance to work with the Dean of the Graduate School of Education and decided to seek her advice about going back to school to pursue a Masters in Higher Education. She knew I already had a master's degree, and asked me to consider applying to the Doctorate program. Noting my apprehension, she said, "Don't worry. I'll help you."

After much encouraging and a lot of convincing by the Dean and faculty, I enrolled in the PhD in Leadership Education program starting that next fall. Soon I was sitting in my first doctoral course, and I was scared out of my mind. The most daunting thought I had was, "It has been 15 years since I was in a classroom. Would I once again feel like I didn't know the 'language'?" In the first class I had, we started the class with introductions. I was happy to see a few people that I recognized. They worked at the university as well. We then went over the syllabus. Not bad, because now I know what a syllabus is. Still very nervous and quite unsure of myself, I decided to stay in the class. Because of the skills and experience gained during my undergrad and master's years (i.e., participating in study groups, utilizing faculty office hours, and accessing resources through the library database), I felt that I belonged. At the end of the semester, I knew I had made the right choice, especially since I got an A-. I enjoyed the courses I was taking, but I did struggle in many of them. Theoretical versus conceptual frameworks, qualitative versus quantitative methods, and Dewey versus Bourdieu, it was hearing a new language all over again. Nonetheless, I successfully completed all course requirements and once again stayed on that Dean's List.

As I now transition into the final phase of the PhD program, I have been confronted with major hurdles. Having succeeded in a guided, structured-environment, it has been difficult for me to transition from being a student to being an independent scholar. I struggle to grasp the concept of the dissertation: how and what to write, how to conduct research – qualitative, quantitative, or mixed methods! Are you kidding me? How am I to know? Where was the course, training or workshop on how to be a write a dissertation, or how to become a researcher? The methodological courses taught me the theory behind different courses but not necessarily how to conduct the research. First generation doctoral students' experiences are quite the same as first generation undergraduates. We still must learn how to navigate the system on our own.

Discussion

Despite coming from different backgrounds and home experiences, Francine and Phitsamay shared many similarities in completing their doctoral studies. First of all, Francine and Phitsamay benefited from having advocates and friends who encouraged and helped them along the way. Phitsamay had her friend Carolyn who had the audacity to push her to believe that a refugee belonged at Harvard and, which in turn, prompted a refugee to have the audacity to ask not just for admission to the esteemed institution, but also for the funding needed to attend. Likewise, Francine got support from her guidance counselor and the Dean who advised her to apply and assisted her with the admission process. The difference between them, though, was that Phitsamay had Carolyn to tell her what help to ask for while Francine did not know how or what to ask for.

Another similarity between Francine's and Phitsamay's experiences was the lack of role models from their own families. Neither knew anyone from their community who was in the academy. The first Asian American professor Phitsamay had was in her junior year at Boston College. She is now the only Lao American tenured faculty in education across the country. Francine has never had an African American woman professor as an instructor.

As a result of their personal experiences, Francine and Phitsamay now consistently work on developing their students' sense of belonging, engagement and involvement on campus. Being first generation, students often struggle to just 'fit in' and learn the academy's language and jargon. For example, a student of color once told Francine that when a professor posted his 'office hours,' the student thought those were the time the professor was NOT to be disturbed because he was working in his office; whereas, one of the Southeast Asian college students said to Phitsamay that they would never go to their professor's office hour because it would be intimidating to sit with a professor for an hour; she said she only had one question. Their students did not realize what office hours are for. This misunderstanding contributes to first-generation students' reluctance to ask for help and to get the support they need. Both of Francine's and Phitsamay's work of helping students is based on the fact that they see themselves in their students. They understand what it means to struggle as a student of color and that is why they work so hard to understand why their students struggle and what supports they can access or create to help the students persist and be more resilient.

Conclusion

As two first generation doctoral students, we have overcome our self-doubts and relied on advocates and allies to navigate through the academy. Based on our experiences, we would make three recommendations to address the barriers and challenges that first-generation students may face. The first recommendation is to have all doctoral programs *provide full financial scholarships for graduate students*. Phitsamay benefitted greatly for the first three years of financial assistance because it took the pressure off from having to work to meet basic needs like housing and food as well as providing her an opportunity to focus on her studies. Francine received tuition credit which is an employee benefit from her employer to pay for doctorate studies.

The second recommendation is to *provide financial support to doctoral students to attend conferences and pursue additional professional development or trainings.* Having funding can create avenues of support, resources, and networks that allows for a more enriched researcher experience. Francine received funding from her Graduate Student Association to attend a regional conference where she was able to receive critical feedback on her research and engage in scholarly conversations with a national network of scholars and colleagues in the field from difference institutions. In this opportunity, Francine was able to see herself as part of a scholarly community.

The third recommendation is to *ensure there is formal mentorship with advanced graduate students and faculty through the first few years.* The chair and dissertation committee help doctoral students pass the finish line; but just as important is the initial three years of the program. Helping first generations make important connections and to understand the doctoral process is essential for retention and graduation of students. Phitsamay and Francine greatly benefitted from the faculty and advanced students in their respective programs. They became a critical friends group who provided critical information on how to navigate a predominantly white institution and insightful feedback on her dissertation ideas to sharpen her analysis and thinking. A distinction to note is that Francine will be the first African American female to graduate from her PhD program in 2020. This speaks for the continued need to support and mentor more first-generation doctoral students to ensure that they succeed in the academy.

References

Coleman, J. S. (1988). Social capital in the creation of human capital. *American Journal of Sociology, 94*, 95–120.

Dunbar, P. L. (1896). We wear the mask. In *Lyrics of lowly life*. Dodd, Mead, and Company.

Rose, H., David, M., & Woodward, D. (1998). An accidental academic. In M. David, M. E. David, & D. Woodward (Eds.), *Negotiating the glass ceiling: Careers of senior women in the academic world* (pp. 101–113). Taylor & Francis.

CHAPTER 9

Enduring: The Misadventures of Navigating a PWI as the Mythical Being Named a Strong Black Woman

Takeshia Pierre

Problem

Isaiah 53 KJV: Chastise Me for Their Peace
No crowd stood by spitting and screaming at me, but I was met with scorn and disgust for speaking up. I wasn't mutilated with any nails to the palms, nor thirty-nine stripes to the body, but I did toil and labor till I didn't recognize myself. I didn't wear a crown of thorns on my head, but I did feel mentally depleted and out of my mind. I carried no cross to Calvary, but I did carry the burden so they wouldn't have to. I've never been a Messiah, but I am born to die for a people, with no resurrection. I'm a black woman.

Research

Matthew 16:26: Gain the World, Lose Your Soul
She smiled from cheek to cheek, hugged her card and rushed over to the tub of markers at the left corner table of the classroom. She wrote "to Jakima," her first name, with a heart drawn over the lowercase letter "I" on the front of the card and added some stickers for additional aesthetics. She and her classmates picked up their Valentine's Day favors and collectively frowned when I broke the news that I would not be coming to class next week since I would be away at a conference.

This was a new reaction from these students. In the last month with apprehension, grumbles, and eventual submission, these middle school students never reacted like *this*. For the past month I began my weekly venture to Abraham Lincoln Middle School where I brought in my idea of fun science activities, but a card and candy seemed to shift their spirits more than painting solar systems and marshmallow bridge building. Something in me knew it wasn't just the candy.

The east side of Gainesville, where Lincoln was located, had the highest concentration of black people and individuals living in poverty. Unbeknownst to many, Lincoln Middle had a rich historical past, but to me, this was the location of the church I frequented. When the opportunity to implement a science program at any middle school within my county opened up, it was my goal to bring my vision there. I had a three-point plan of how I was going to target, intervene, and build African American middle school students to become the scholars I knew they could be. This was a genuine gesture that soon developed into a researcher jackpot. Alachua county, where Lincoln was located, was home to the largest achievement gap between black and white students in the state. Lincoln was also the only middle school that did not have another academic program running concurrently, which meant my study would be prime baseline data. The urgency from the college for me to get cleared to collect data intensified, and so did my uneasiness about the current approach to my program.

Hypothesis

2 Timothy 1:7 NKJV: Of Power and a Sound Mind – Black Women and Anxiety

"Why is this always happening," I thought, massaging the unavoidable tight grip forming in the pit of my stomach. This reaction increased overtime, never to be outwardly discussed with anyone, but internally it became a physiological battleground. For the past three months I felt physically barricaded, my mind using excessive force to stop any writing process relevant to my program at Lincoln. Following my encounter with the students on Valentine's Day, my habits were avoidant of anyone and anything that sought to remind me of my after-school science program and getting the paperwork to begin researching the students at Lincoln. It occurred to me a few weeks following the holiday, that this was the moment students began to feel *seen*. "Why are we a part of this program and not the other kids?" asked one of the students. "Because you're all special Demarkus, I responded back." This conversation happened in January, but it seemed that February 14th marked the day students truly began to feel this way.

I started using the telephone application I intended to use with my students called Headspace to clear my mind and deal with what I thought was anxiety. At that moment, I knew I felt odd about my program, but what about it?

Experiment

Matthew 26:25: Re/De-Colonization – Surely You Don't Mean Me?
Eunice Rivers Laurie is often left out of the Tuskegee experiment story. She was a black nurse who recruited and followed up with the black male participants and knowingly failed to help treat them of syphilis when a cure became available. I was always told that the Tuskegee experiment was the prime example of how not to conduct a study.

"You feel like you're oppressing the students Takeshia," said Dr. Bondy. Concerned that mid-semester I was not completing assignments related to Lincoln for my qualitative analysis course, the professor, Dr. Bondy, suggested we talk via telephone during spring break. Tears began to stream from my eyes as things began to make sense. After a month of failing to submit a paper about my study, I didn't quite understand why I *couldn't* submit. "Are you treating these students as subjects?" I thought as I stared into my phone screen following our conversation. "Am I the black liaison to usher in oppression through this program?"

A light went off. That semester I had been taking a Critical Race Theory (CRT) course that began to challenge what I felt was progressive. "Racism is permanent" read one of the tenets, and the education system was not immune but actually the root of where forms of systemic oppression occurred. "Take on the role of a journal reviewer and critique an article within your field" said Dr. Busey. "This shouldn't be bad," I thought, "I've dealt with oppression my entire academic career." I stared at the article selection for two days and watched the cursor on the Microsoft Word document appear and disappear. Similar to the incidences with typing my paper for Dr. Bondy, the stomach knot reappeared. I minimized the document and completed another assignment.

Data Collection

Psalm 24:5–6: Vindication for Them Too, Lincoln High
"Lincoln Middle School used to be a high school," said Mr. Gunther, a former Lincoln Middle School Blue Terrier and current principal of Abraham Lincoln Middle. Learning about the impacts of integration nationally, particularly the calling for the expulsion of several African American educators, and the subsequent closure of African American serving schools, it would make sense that Lincoln was not an exception of the unfortunate byproducts of desegregation. The school was forced to close down in 1970 and black students were forced

to bus to the west side of town to integrate into the all-white school named Gainesville High School (GHS).

Preparing a manuscript for my Critical Race Theory course, speaking with community members who went to Lincoln High became a surprisingly fruitful opportunity to not only learn more about Lincoln's history, but provide a counter-story to the master-narrative often told about the closure of Lincoln (Solórzano & Yosso, 2002). After reading much of a book called "We can do it" that was authored from a viewpoint of an elderly white male, I felt responsible to truly look at the case that allowed for the closure of Lincoln High School, and report the true feelings of the black community redacted from periodicals and stories printed about the closure of Lincoln similar to "We can do it." My bible study member Ms. Cat asked around her neighborhood and called me when she got in contact with a Lincoln High alum that would speak with me. "Takeshia, every first Thursday of the month, Lincoln High alumni meet at the center near downtown. Ask for Mr. Brown," she said Wednesday afternoon, a day prior to the monthly meeting. This seemed like a sign from God to attend.

The next day I came a few minutes early to get a good seat. I introduced myself to the group and they opened with prayer before reading their previous meeting minutes. They talked of plans for the fall banquet and reunion weekend events, prices for venues, and a proposed price to charge alum for tickets. "Remember we can't call it a picnic, said one of the members. It would upset many people because when they'd [klansman] go lynchin' they used to call it a picnic, meaning 'pick-a-nigga.' Call it a bar-b-q."

One thing I left the meeting knowing that there was a pride that racism couldn't kill. Mr. Brown told me of how there were many Lincoln High alum alive and holding onto their school memorabilia. He was interested in displaying their school's artifacts in a memory room at Lincoln Middle, but many reasonably wanted to hold onto their old high school memories. In the year 2020, it would mark the 50th year of the closure of Lincoln High school, and a dream for the alum would be to build a wall at Lincoln with the names of all the alumni. While joyful memories were often expressed of their high school days, with various people describing football games, pep rallies, and old classmates, I also picked up on a major burden they had carried for nearly 50 years – they never felt vindicated. Many of the group had given their oral histories to individuals interested in Lincoln in the past, but none of the alumni at the meeting attended the integrated schools, because they'd graduated by 1969. Fortunately, I was put in contact with a man named Richard Mays, a former student of Lincoln High and GHS and a schoolteacher named Mrs. Florence Myles who taught at both schools.

Galatians 4:7: Mental Slaves Obey the Master Narrative; No Longer a Slave

Similar to the collective pride shown by the alumni, another narrative arose from the closure of Lincoln High – stories of injustice, robbery, trauma, and regret. "Why did we have to lose our school, our pride, and be humiliated? If I had to do it again, I would not have fought for integration" he said. Mr. Mays was not alone. The following week, Mrs. Florence Myles mirrored the same thoughts. Individuals in the community believed integration would bring forth a positive influence in the black community, but as many have witnessed, the aggressive climate they entered following legislation and the state of their community disparities, proved a hefty price to pay for "equality."

"I'm fighting back tears. I remember one of our beloved teachers transferred over to GHS and died of a stroke because it was just too much," Mrs. Myles said. Like her old high school teacher, the racist climate many African American students and educators endured in desegregated hallways proved too stressful. Daily they were harassed with racial slurs and violent behavior by whites following integration. Racism remained unaltered, but the promise of a progressive future led to the dismantling of a pride and also the souls of black people, including those living in Gainesville. The trauma from the closure of Lincoln High still lingers in the community and justice was never served.

Analysis

Acts 9:18: And the Scales Fell from Her Eyes

Since I was a child in elementary school, I was taught the scientific method. My first science project was titled "Which Nail Polish Color Dries the Fastest?" The purpose for the experiment – choosing to test between the colors red and blue – was to help make life for the working woman easier. If a woman was in a rush to get to her job in the morning, I explained, she had to know which nail polish color dried quick enough to make it to work on time, while not missing out on being beautiful. After running my experiment, observing, and collecting my data, the color blue won.

Within the second semester of my PhD program, the scientific method became a lot more difficult. Now my experiment had a soul and my data was based on a living body. Historically there was a held belief that Black people had no soul. When I considered the three-fifths compromise, it made me realize just how little has changed in society following this "compromise." The vision for my science program was coined holistic, but I had to question how to capture the wholeness of a child when an education system built on white supremacy considered them two-fifths short of a person?

The education system suddenly became robotic to me. Control their setting, alter their behaviors, delete their personhood in the name of science. My color gave me access to their communities and my consistency built their trust. I soon learned that every token still pays a price. The moment I received access to these students, the homogenous racial groups suddenly became interesting to white colleagues, and I was the shoe-in to access these Black children. I found myself protecting Lincoln from research colonization. Researcher after researcher suddenly became interested in their demographics, questioning how many students attended my program to get enough of a sense of the sample size. I learned the cost of bearing the burden of a community and stopping to consider their whole being – something I thought would be second nature to a top university known to develop educators that were considered the best and the brightest.

Consequently, I bought into the savior mentality. My goal was to pull this community out of a hole 50 years deep, even as I was searching for guidance myself as a first-generation student. Ten years of navigating a predominantly white institution (PWI) as a student and employee taught me to research and intervene at all costs, even at the expense of a community's wellbeing. Get up, kill, eat.

The academy taught me that in their minds, it didn't matter how Black children were handled. Since no one really cared to go to the "hood," it was enough that someone even took an interest in them. So I took up a cross. Witnessing the killing of a tradition, the stealing of a narrative, and the destruction of a legacy, I had to name the true thief in the night, seeking to devour this community. It was white supremacy masked in the education system. I was introduced to the new methods of colonization in the form of research. This came with the breaking of Black bodies, as the education system toasted with their blood. Including my own.

I was posed with an inner battle and "double mindedness" and double consciousness proved too much for one soul (James 1:8 The King James Version; Du Bois, 1903/1968). My inner being was challenged with the decision to progress and oppress, or self-sabotage in order to protect. Do I quickly turnaround a paper for publication or do nothing and risk my scholarship? The problem was my heart made the decision before my mind could even respond. Anxiety kept me from moving forward, but deep down I believe my soul was pushing back.

As a Black woman I was already placed in a position as the "single mother" to "rear" these students, give them firm words, and pose as the Harriet Tubman of my day to guide them in the right direction to scientific genius. But I had to be still, reevaluate, and do no harm to my students. My north star was my faith. God did cover me. I was able to postpone the completion of my coursework in order to identify methods to truly develop an educational program that will build and not further oppress my students.

I've made a stern decision to combat the narrative society has made for me, and how to handle this community. While there have been sneers and snickers from my colleagues due to the lack of publications coming out of a research gold-mine, I made the decision that my "strength" is not to be perverted to procreate with oppression for publications recklessly done through the use of Black bodies. If the Lord is my strength, I couldn't keep quiet about my lack. If I believed the whole world was in His hands, I had to stop thinking there was blood on my own. I had eyes to see what white supremacy didn't – the beauty from ashes that were in the face and words of wisdom of Lincoln students, past and present.

I had to interrogate my need to ignore my body, silently lose my mind, and pollute my soul. It was what society taught me to be, strong and indestructible which I learned meant to ignore the personhood and internal health of a Black woman. I'm taking ownership of our narrative. I am not a robot, I am not indestructible, I am not the Strong Tower, nor the rock to stand on. The indestructible strong Black woman is a mythical creature. We feel, we nurture, we cry, we love, we study, we pray, we're human.

Conclusion

Romans 12:1: A Living Sacrifice

I've chosen to honor my students and their community by centering their race and culture to collaboratively build their education. I plan to change the narrative of the subsequent re-segregation of Lincoln Middle by creating counter-spaces to promote and nurture healthy identity development within my students. My goal is to hear the perspectives of Lincoln students about how I can make their experiences with science interesting, rather than imposing my ideas as a researcher. Building on their knowledge, beliefs, and racial identity can promote change. The grandchildren of Lincoln High School alumni will have to be the solution for the disparity I long to chase away. History will not repeat itself for another 50 years.

As for me, I learned that there *is* life after death and a sacrifice that does not reify the myth of a strong Black woman. An exchange of plans and subsequent death needed to occur for the advancement of this community – a death of my plans, for God's. I am taking back the meaning of what it is to be sacrificial, where I acknowledge that I am the vessel and personification of a sacrifice – but I am leaning on supernatural strength that was never mine to begin with. An exchange of my strength has occurred, for God's. So here is my body, as a sacrifice.

References

Du Bois, W. E. B. (1968). *The souls of Black folk: Essays and sketches.* Johnson Reprint Corp. (Original work published 1903)

Solórzano, D. G., & Yosso, T. J. (2002). Critical race methodology: Counter-storytelling as an analytical framework for education research. *Qualitative Inquiry, 8*(1), 23–44.

CHAPTER 10

Smile Now, Cry Later: Navigating Structures of Inequality in Academia through Resistance, Resilience, and Humor in Our Women of Color Writing Group

Gloria Negrete-Lopez, Lisa S. Palacios and Alejandra I. Ramírez

Introduction

We[1]: As first-generation women of color doctoral students, we intentionally come together to carve out a space from which we resist and move forward in our graduate studies. Meeting through this writing group allows us to find solace and joy in writing and research. We often experience and internalize hurtful narratives or comments within our university, but take the famous idiom of 'smile now, cry later'[2] as a way of staying critical while humanizing our individual and collective experiences. 'Smile now, cry later' is especially relevant for us as working class people of color. The corresponding twin masks, one happy, one sad, are popular in our communities, easily found in sticker machines at the grocery store, as common tattoos, and airbrushed on t-shirts at the swap-meet. We carry this symbol and what it represents into our experiences as first-generation women of color graduate students, just as we carry our communities' stories with us, and we are reminded to stay true to who we are despite calls for assimilation.

The Women of Color (WOC) Graduate Writing Group[3] has served as a place to express our frustration with institutionalized white supremacy and "gate keepers." The three of us (Gloria, Lisa, and Alejandra – scholars with similar working class backgrounds) have reinscribed what graduate student writing groups can and ought to be. Our group became a space to share community resources and laughter – making dissertating pleasurable. Writing is difficult enough but when you analyze and critique institutional practices and policies – the very roots of academia – your work is met with resistance. We are WOC writing for predominantly white audiences, audiences who benefit from the classist, cisgender, white, ableist, and hetero-partriarchal university. Thus, to critique these oppressive practices and policies of an institution is an affront to them and, as they might read us, an affront to our and their livelihood.

Here, we detail our resistance through laughter and our resilience to institutional violence. We document only a few of the historical traumas and the institutional violences of graduate school in conversation. Despite the trauma we have each faced, we remain committed to our goals of finishing and graduating from our respective departments.

Whose Group? Our Group!: The Writing Group Space

We: Our writing practice creates a space of resistance and resilience. Engaging in this collaborative writing praxis, we speak what remains unspoken in the classroom; we bear the brunt of professionalism, another name for whiteness, classism, ableism, and heteropatriarchy. Our bodies and scholarship are marked with that wounding.

Lisa: I don't know where my confidence comes from. But, I think it comes from our discussions. Especially our meetings and the sessions we have had together and all of the writing we have done together and in the acknowledgement that there is an obvious need for more emphasis on physical spaces for students of color. People of Color [PoC] exist in this world and PoC that go to this university – who are paying for this experience – deserve spaces to build community and confidence. We deserve to have spaces and a voice and we deserve to be ourselves on this campus. Spaces that are free of microaggressions.

Alejandra: I too understand feeling stubborn, speaking up, and how the writing group helped you (Lisa) to do that. I like that y'all feel and think similarly. You have to be careful about who is listening to you when you critique the institution. But anger can be generative, it can "translate pain into knowledge," and "open up the world" to do more and be more (Ahmed, 2012, p. 171).

Even in and out of the writing group space, when we email or text, our group is a space where we can be critical of institutional injustices – open and honest about our critiques. It's been important to be in the group and get everyone's feedback and Andrea's feedback, and be able to voice my process comfortably.

Gloria: The writing group is a space where we can be vocal about what we are struggling with, such as writer's block. I also feel like I can be funny and I can say things that are honest and off the cuff along with laughing with all of you. More importantly, our writing group is a shared common space where not only do I feel safe but I can express myself about how I deal with academia or anything. This space allows me to be open and laugh about school.

Smile Now: Humor as Resistance

We: Imagine a reality show that documents the lives of graduate students! The camera crew follows us during our daily activities across campus.

SCENE 1: The camera films one of us in a classroom lecturing and attempting to joke around with the students using some pop culture reference in the hopes of making them laugh (or to at least appear somewhat "cool"). Instead, the camera captures students yawning and unimpressed.

SCENE 2: A different grad student comes out of a professor's office hours holding back tears. She says "another great meeting with Professor X. Excuse me as I step into my office to write down some notes." Then, we see a closed office door with the caption "muffled crying sounds."

We laugh because it's true! We find relief in our communal laughter as women of color in the academic struggle.

Gloria: When I began grad school I kept hearing people say that we should view professors as our future colleagues. We learn that, at the same time, they may wield their power and authority to remind us that we are mere students. I see humor as a way for me to resist and make light of the educational and institutional violences that happen. I cannot be angry all the time because it is exhausting and taxing so, for me, laughing is self-preservation. If I dwell on it for too long it will make me depressed.

Lisa: We have to be able to laugh at all that we've endured. We have to smile now *and* cry later. I'm sure some people don't connect to that statement and wonder "What is that? What does it mean?" In response, we'd say "Didn't you go to the grocery store as a kid and get those stickers?" or "Didn't you see *American Me*?" They would not get it. I'm sure some would probably say, "I've seen *American Me* but for an anthropology class" or something like that. It's not something most non-PoC grow up watching in their households.

That's something I tend to do – keep away from non-PoC who don't have historical trauma – like, I don't want to enjoy things with you. You didn't struggle and neither did your people. They are so far removed from that experience. They do not deserve me or my humor because they do not understand the trauma behind it. Or, they pretend to understand it. On top of figuring out what we're going to be dedicating our lives to in grad school we have to manage how to deal with microaggressions.

Alejandra: The argument we are trying to make is that laughter is a survival mechanism, a way of "talking back," to heal, to resist (Souza, 2001). Scholars have made similar critiques of the institution (Ahmed, 2012; Cordova, 1998; Gutiérrez, 2012) but for us as graduate students, it is about how we are able to laugh through it. For many of us, our professional lives, our futures, and our families' futures are at stake—our mental health and our physical health depends on being able to express joy. We want to see a better version of the university. We are trying to do something positive, and there is pleasure and a willingness to laugh.

I feel really isolated in grad school since there aren't a lot of single mothers. I have kids to feed and they don't have insurance. But I find joy outside the institution with my kids and niece. I get a lot of pleasure just sitting at home watching dumb shows and laughing with them. They teach me more about life and myself than any institution or any book has. They remind me how things can be simple. I can be myself, and I'm at ease.

I like that our writing group shares in various identities and experiences, which helps us understand the jokes we make about how crazy the university is, how violent it is, and folks like us are looking at it for what it is. It's also a relief to be able to talk about it in writing group, and think, "yea, these women, 'they get it.'" I am able to trust and joke about difficult moments, and we make ourselves feel better, and that is resistance. The whole time the research institution is trying to understand our experience, but we understand it better than it understands us. It wishes it could understand us. Comedy, just like any other art, emerges from your experience and so this happens to be our experience. I think that there is a lot of recovery and healing that happens through laughter and then you feel a little better and it feels cathartic, kind of like crying.

Gloria: Because we are normally the punchline of a joke, right? Y'all (institutions) have already done so much to me and my community along with all these microaggressions about stuff in the classroom. No, we are not going to be the punchline of a joke anymore!

Cry Later: Institutional Violence and Scars Left Behind

We: As Women of Color feminists that inhabit various fields at the same institution, we see the importance of feminist solidarity in this current political climate and our geographical location in the Southwestern borderlands region. Despite our campus promoting its designations as a "Land-Grant University," a "Hispanic Serving Institution," and it's "pride" in having the largest Native American student population in the region, in our experience, this institution falsely promotes a commitment to diversity.

Lisa: There are a bunch of non-Native people in my field and they are not comfortable dealing with racism or 'other-isms.' There was an incident I had with a supervisor who was trying to take my picture in the lab, which I was not comfortable with. It is straight up wrong to take my photo without my consent. My issue had nothing to do with anthropological or archeological theory or method, it has nothing to do with that – it was about ethics. The Edward Curtis narrative of Natives frozen in time needs to be undone – it's 2019 after all. But Natives are still revered for our aesthetic qualities in academia. We have no agency over our own bodies.

Despite how outrageous the things that have been said to me are, the responses are never "wow that WAS really racist" or "they took advantage of you" – it is never that. It's always that case that something was wrong with me. My resistance and my testimony in these instances is what's most offensive to them. I think other students of color and other Native students that enter my field are broken down and they're forced to have the mentality of "I just need to get through this," or "It is hard. I hate this! I just need to get through it." They are experiencing trauma but they're silent about it. But that is not the road I've taken. My frame of mind is, 'It is my money' and it is my tribe's money, I don't think that they would appreciate their money contributing to the marginalization of their own people.

My field needs to understand that these experiences contribute to the retention rates of Native students in the field of anthropology, archaeology, and specifically at my university. Diversity and inclusion is not through being told we're 'wrong' for standing up for ourselves and for valuing things like consent as important. They can't tell me that other students of color or other Native students just throw agency out the window because we're anomalies in the discipline.

Alejandra: I remember reading Chela Sandoval's *Methodology of the Oppressed* (2000) for graduate seminar because we were supposed to present on a methodology that informed our research trajectory, and I remember the professor saying, "If you want to make anything of yourself in this field then you will have to learn how to assimilate." It was really messed up to hear a man of color who is supposed to be an ally tell me something like that in the middle of my first semester, in front of my cohort. I responded with, "That's the fucken problem." I knew from then on that I was not where I thought I was, because I had higher expectations of graduate school. I was up close and personal with racist institutional violence. I've heard people yell offensive things at me on the street, but these institutions and the kind of power they have is scary.

Gloria: We have been discussing how academia views us as unruly and undisciplined subjects for speaking out. We are threatening when we decide to confront racism. What does it mean when they are telling us to assimilate? For me personally, it is obvious from listening to that and hearing someone telling us to assimilate that the expectation is that we are supposed to change ourselves.

I have to go back to that first day of graduate school and the university-wide graduate student orientation in 2014. I will never forget the president of the graduate council saying, "This isn't your father's graduate school experience and this isn't your brother's graduate school experience." I looked around the room and saw people nod in agreement. I didn't nod; instead, I sat there in disbelief. I am a first-generation graduate student – there is no one else in my family with this experience! But no one really wants to discuss the structural inequality within graduate school or within the communities that we are a part of as graduate students. We simply cannot ignore the way class differences are embedded in that. For many of us, our class experience dictates how we are coming into the institution. We come into graduate school thinking that we want to improve our quality of life and help our families and provide them with something. We want to be "this professional" and yet we're sold this fabricated lie.

All of a sudden, I find myself in this huge debt (student loans are necessary to live!). I'm supposed to help out my family when, in actuality, this is making me more impoverished. Many of my classmates are coming from these middle class backgrounds and they don't have to worry as to how they are going to support their families and they don't send money back for them so that they can pay their bills and have food in their refrigerator. I do not have the privilege of knowing what it is like to focus on my scholarship. Professors say, "You will never have this much free time when you are a professor." And I say to myself "what? ... I'M EXHAUSTED ALREADY! Because I have been going to school and working since I was 15 and now I'm 32." For some like myself it takes us a bit longer to write. For example, instead of focusing on the editing for this piece, I am holding space for my mother as she tearfully explains that

FIGURE 10.1   Left to right: Andrea (facilitator), Lisa, Gloria, and Alejandra

she needs economic support. While class analysis is just a theory for others, it is something that I live.

We: The university has a responsibility and is indebted to the communities that surround the area, yet undergraduate and graduate students are forced to confront interpersonal and institutional violence that is not legible by many because it happens behind closed doors, in the labs that we work in, and in our classrooms at the hands of law enforcement. As first-generation students and as women of color scholars, we refuse to stay silent any longer. Ultimately, We will have the last laugh!

Notes

1. Our writing style in this essay has been informed by a conversational style present in the work of Gloria Anzaldúa *Entrevistas* (2000) and Malea Powell et al. (2014). As we reflected on how institutional life has impacted us individually, we grappled with a writing style that would best represent our process thus far. We began writing individually, then meeting at coffee shops, and finally recording our conversation and transcribing. Our voice was heard here. It is through a back and forth, conversational exchange, that our voices and laughter ring collectively.
2. Also, the title of a 1966 song by Sunny & the Sunliners.
3. We are brought together biweekly by Dr. Andrea Holm, who facilitates our WoC graduate writing group out of the Writing Skills Improvement Program at the University of Arizona. Dr. Holm offers us a safe space where we can share our experiences in academia with one another and helps us incorporate these experiences into our scholarship.

References

Ahmed, S. (2012). *On being included: Racism and diversity in institutional life*. Duke University Press.

Anzaldúa, G. E., & Keating, A. (2000). *Interviews/Entrevistas*. Routledge.

Cordova, T. (1998). Power and knowledge: Colonialism in the academy. In C. Trujillo (Ed.), *Living Chicana theory* (pp. 17-45). Third Woman Press.

Gutiérrez y Muhs, G. (2012). *Presumed incompetent the intersections of race and class for women in academia*. University Press of Colorado.

Powell, M., Levy D., Riley-Mukavetz, A., Brooks-Gillies, M., Novotny, M., & Fisch-Ferguson, J. (2014). Our story begins here: constellating cultural rhetorics. *Enculturation: A journal of rhetoric, writing, and culture*. University of South Carolina Press.

Sandoval, C. (2000). *Methodology of the oppressed* (Theory out of Bounds, Vol. 18). University of Minnesota Press.

Souza, C. (2001). Esta risa no es de loca. In A. Morales, P. Zavella, N. Alarcón, R. Behar, L. Acevedo, C. Alvarez, ... C. Souza (Eds.), *Telling to live Latina feminist testimonios* (pp. 115–122). Duke University Press.

CHAPTER 11

A One-Sided Conversation with Academia

Joy Cobb

I am sitting in the basement of the library with my head in my hands, trying to figure out how to explain my doctoral experience. Over the last three years, I believe I have had a late-night writing session on each floor of this seven-story building. This time is different, but no less challenging. The task is to articulate a moment that captures my experience as a Black, first-generation, female, graduate student from a limited-income upbringing. I realize that I am having a difficult time because my story is not about a particular moment. It is about a state of being. A constant uneasiness.

Growing up, I was unaware of the odds against me. I grew up in a loving home where trying my best, and behaving in school were my primary responsibilities. Though my educational trajectory flies in the face of statistics, school was the arena where I performed best. My mother recalls with amusement, my five-year-old proclamation that I had the "good-est and best-est" brain in my kindergarten class. Since then, I have continued to perform well in class-related tasks, but the confident five-year-old of the past, was not prepared for the hidden aspects of higher education.

A Message from the Tower

My first thoughts of graduate school came during my final year of undergrad. This was four years before I would enroll in my master's program. A professor started a short one-sided conversation consisting of the words: "THIS IS GRADUATE LEVEL WORK." I was flattered yet confused about what to do with this information. These five words scrawled in red on the bottom right corner of the last page of a graded assignment represent the only professional or faculty advice I have received about graduate studies prior to enrolling in my current doctoral program. I still have the assignment tucked away because although I had no clue what to do with those words, I did know that the recognition of my potential was powerful. As the only child of a Black, working-class, high school graduate, single mother; graduate school represented more time and more money. Neither of which seemed to be at my disposal.

My chance encounter with the professor of the prophetic five words came as the result of a senior year major change to sociology. It was a field I was familiar with from general education courses, and it turned out to be a great fit. I grasped the concepts with ease and found most of the topics interesting. By the end of the program, I wanted to be a researcher. I knew that graduate school was the answer, but I had no idea how to get there. I came from a working-class family comprised of factory and county government workers living paycheck-to-paycheck. I am still surprised that as a sociologist, my professor did not consider the social and cultural capital needs of the lone black female student in his class. I often wonder what a simple "hey let's talk after class" would have meant for my life's journey. But he didn't ask, and I didn't know to ask.

For years I had received messages that college was the key to a good life. I believed that by following the formula of doing well in high school and graduating from college that a good job would come naturally. What I found was that this approach does not work as well for students in liberal arts and social sciences. Students who pursue professional fields graduate with a marker of what they are to become. Those who major in engineering become engineers. Nursing majors become nurses. Teaching majors become teachers. With an undergraduate degree in Sociology, I did not feel prepared to become anything.

Many poor, Black students come to higher education to pursue high profile fields with high earning potential. This was not my path. My talents are concentrated in soft skills, and I care about people and their experiences. I enjoy exchanging ideas. I understand many technical concepts, but my strengths do not lie in their application. As a poor Black student in humanities, graduation felt like I was about to be swallowed up by an unknown world. As always, my family was supportive of anything I wanted to do. However, support was not the issue. I needed guidance, but I lacked the understanding to articulate the "lack" that I was feeling.

Today I don't know if I should empathize with my younger self or be angry with her for not figuring it out. I was a smart girl. For the most part, my college journey was a solo endeavor. There weren't many formal conversations about college growing up. It was understood that I was going, but I'm not sure if any of us thought about how it was going to happen. This meant that I went with the basics of what I knew. I applied. I was accepted. I graduated.

Almost twenty years later, history is poised to repeat itself.

My interest in graduate school was reignited after learning that a friend of mine was pursuing a master's degree in higher education online. We were good friends, so I got to see her work and ask questions. Proximity gave way to possibility. Through this friendship, I was able to see someone who looked like me and who shared the same intellectual capacity, navigating a space I longed to be in. My renewed interest came with its share of self-doubt. In my search for programs, I limited my search to schools that did not require the Graduate Records Exam (GRE).

I researched reputable online master's programs and enrolled. I was aware that there were many brick and mortar schools that I could apply to but had a tough time understanding how I, as a working adult with an apartment, a car payment, and modest student loans, was supposed to stop my life and enroll fulltime in school again. I knew of assistantship positions, but I viewed them as far too competitive. I also did not believe that I had what it took to be anyone's assistant. I felt that I didn't possess the requisite knowledge, experience, or ability to actually do anything other than what I was already doing. I wasn't involved in college organizations or research. My goal during undergrad was to perform well and not mess up the opportunity. I viewed graduate school as another place to perform, not as an opportunity to learn and develop. Through my professional experience in higher education, I realize that I was entirely wrong.

Where Am I? And How Did I End up Here?

My story to this point has been a tale of wandering and wondering. That did not change when I took the leap into a doctoral program. I found myself engaged in the same one-sided conversation with the academy again. I showed up eager, willing, and able. Apparently, I brought the same doubt and invisibility from my undergraduate experience. I definitely did not fly under the radar in class. My understanding of the material, outspoken demeanor, and quick wit definitely attracted attention. A scan of my academic record shows nothing surprising; stellar marks across the board. In my previous academic experiences, grades would have served as a testament of a job well done. Yet, there was a feeling that I could not shake. A feeling that some of my classmates knew something that I did not know or that there were experiences that I was not privy to.

The confirmation of my suspicions came in spurts. The first was a group text of congratulations on a classmate's recent publication. Then again, after learning that another classmate was turning a class paper into a research project with a faculty member. These accomplishments amongst my closest classmates made me wonder what I was doing wrong or even worse that maybe I just wasn't as good at this scholarship thing as they were. My only claims to fame were enthusiastic agreements during class conversations and consistent passing grades on papers and assignments. Outside of the standard curriculum, I was having difficulty with not being seen.

The irony of not being seen as one of two Black students in my cohort is not lost on me. It occurred to me early that I am the only person in my program who holds the particular combinations of identity attributes that I find most salient to my lived experience. I was not initially concerned by not finding a reflection of self in the classroom via faculty or classmates. There are others who are first-generation, black, from limited-income households, but they each hold an identity of privilege that emboldens their interactions and their work. My first-generation classmates are white, and my Black classmate is a second-generation student who attended suburban schools. I did not enter my program with a sense that I naturally belonged there. My arguments in written work have been critiqued for being too passive. I often hedge my assertions with "could be" and "possibly" because I do not have the audacity to consider myself an expert.

This Is Graduate-Level Work!

In the same way that the accomplishments of classmates began to emerge, so have opportunities to make my scholarly presence known. I received feedback on an assignment with the notation to take some time to meet with the professor to discuss how to turn my research into a journal submission. Eureka! I am years removed from my disappointing undergraduate faculty acknowledgment, but this recognition came at a time when I had grown tired of sitting on the sidelines. More importantly, it came with an invitation. I was finally invited in.

Since the faculty invitation, I have answered multiple calls for proposals, engaged in research with faculty, and begun to consider my scholarly and professional contributions to higher education seriously. Having been exposed to American boot-strap rhetoric, I am somewhat ashamed of my previous passivity in exploring my options beyond what was immediately accessible. I was attempting to pursue this degree alone. Graduate work is independent in nature, but it is not enough to simply be a good student. My success in primary and secondary education came from making high marks and staying out of the way. Scholarship requires collaboration and making yourself known.

I have learned these lessons. I am finally finding my way as a scholar, and using my pitfalls and new understanding to inform the next generation. I've learned that sponsorship is difficult to obtain organically when you don't share the same background as those in power. Common language and common interest turn into personal relationships. So much knowledge and insight are gained through casual conversations with faculty. For me, these conversations are still difficult, but I recognize their importance as I continue to take the initiative to be seen and heard.

CHAPTER 12

Just What Is a First-Generation Chinese Male Immigrant and College Student Doing in a *Nice* Field Like Teacher Education?

Lin Wu

"Thank you so much for so carefully choosing our readings and for all the awesome class discussions. I will always try to incorporate Paulo Freire and bell hooks into my teaching. And thank you for teaching from your heart, I will try to do the same."

When I read this feedback on my course evaluation, my eyes welled up. It was bittersweet, not just for the kind words, or because it was the last time I taught the Multicultural Education course in the Secondary Teacher Education Program (STEP) at a predominately White institution (PWI). Rather, it was because it showed how far I have come in my personal and professional development in regard to living and teaching about diversity.

According to Sleeter (2017), Whiteness is pervasive in US teacher education programs' (TEPS') structures, curricula, faculty, administrator, student populations, and field placements. By "Whiteness" she meant the overwhelming dominance of White (re)presentations and prevailing points of reference. The realities tend to ensure that instructors of color in TEPs will encounter "pushback" or resistance in various formats because of race, or ethnicity, or gender, or language, or social class, and a combination of these. Another constraining factor is the assumption that these instructors of color will automatically be experts on diversity and therefore expected to be responsible for teaching courses on multicultural education (Gay & Howard, 2000). Although many educational scholars have illuminated the struggles, resilience, wisdom, and success of teacher educators of color (Ladson-Billings, 2005; Picower & Kohli, 2017), few have researched the intersections of race, ethnicity, immigration, culture, and college status at the same time. Using *AsianCrit* (Iftikar & Museus, 2018) as the guiding framework, I present three counterstories about my personal experiences as a first-generation Chinese male immigrant and college student working in teacher education.

Counterstory I: Breaking the Bamboo Ceiling

I began my doctorate in Multicultural Education at the beginning of the 2015–2016 academic year at a PWI in the Pacific Northwest. Previously I had served a predominately working-class Latinx community in the Southwest for seven years as a teacher and principal. I naively assumed that my working experiences would help me quickly secure good financial and unreserved personal support from the College of Education. After all, this was a huge tier-one research university. Yet it took me one year to obtain a graduate teaching assistant (TA) position in the STEP at the College of Education. When I stepped into the orientation meeting with all the new hires, I quickly noticed that I was "statistical anomaly" since I was the *only* male of color of any kind. My intersectional identities as a first-generation Chinese male immigrant and doctoral student broke the STEP's bamboo ceiling in its TA hiring history. Being the "only one" was just the beginning. My experiences as a TA and my identities were impacted by multiple inequities embedded throughout the STEP.

Shortly after I started working in the program, the 2016 US presidential election happened. As I observed different communities of color (including my own) grappling with the chaos that resulted, I was reminded of the violence that Chinese immigrants experienced along the US West Coast in the 1800s. When I returned to work the day after the election, I noticed that many students, especially those of color, seemed to be agonized. The instructor (a White female) of my class and I shared our thoughts and feelings, listened to students' concerns, and then moved on to the lesson we had previously planned. By the end of the class, students accomplished their assigned tasks. Later I learned from colleagues that when the same instructor (with a different TA) taught a different group of students in the afternoon, she started the class checking in with students regarding the election. One student of color criticized the instructor for not thoroughly analyzing the election, and attributed her failure to her Whiteness. This led to heated arguments and the abrupt dismissal of the class.

Subsequently, I was called into the program director's office to help clarify details of this incident. Besides telling my mostly White supervisors that I was not physically present during this incident, I expressed my empathy for the student of color and willingness to help the class move forward. Later that night, I received a phone call from the program director. She started the conversation in a casual, friendly tone. When I asked her the solution for the incident, she replied, "We decided to send you into that class next week." I thought about this decision and replied politely, "I am willing to help with the situation, but I don't feel comfortable going into that class to help ease the tension." She replied immediately, "Well, I don't give a shit about how you feel. You're gonna help us with it."

After hearing this response, I realized that there was no point for me to argue with her when the institutional power allowed her to dictate what I would do and not take my concern or well-being as a TA and doctoral student into consideration. In an outwardly calm tone I replied, "I will go, but only as a TA, not a mediator for class tensions."

In US society, Asian Americans are often perceived as model minorities who have "made it." The incident I just described did not make me feel like I had "made it." Instead, it felt more like exploitation! By sending me to the class as a mediator for racial tensions, the White program director used her power to proxy me as an Asian immigrant. Her action reproduced the "middle men" dilemma historically imposed upon Asian Americans to undermine African Americans' pursuit of justice and thus uphold White supremacy (Takaki, 1998). Meanwhile, the decision made by the "leaders" not only demonstrated their incapacity to resolve racial conflicts among White instructors and students of color, but also perpetuated institutionalized racism against a graduate student of color. It was apparent to me how race, immigration, and power came into play in this situation. How I was treated was reflective of the rampant racism before, during, and after the presidential election. But little could I foresee that this was merely a prelude to more difficult lessons I would learn in the STEP in the next two years.

Counterstory II: Unveiling the Mask of Whiteness

At the start of a Multicultural Education course in Summer 2017, Charleena Lyles, a pregnant African American mother of four, was murdered by two White male Seattle police officers. As a lead instructor for the course, I found my colleagues (one White female lead instructor and one White female TA) and myself in a Catch-22 situation, since many students expected us to discuss this issue yet none of us could speak from personal experiences of police brutality. But we knew it was important that we address this murder in class.

As the White lead instructor expressed her sympathy for Charleena's family, a few White female students joined the conversation and asked if we should spend the entire class discussing this issue. Before our team responded, four female students of color walked out of the classroom one-by-one. Realizing they had spent about 10 minutes talking without any input from peers of color, some White female students started to cry. My colleagues asked them to process their feelings through silent journaling. I stepped outside to check-in with the female students of color, only to find out that none of them wanted to speak with our team. After class, my colleagues and I communicated with the program director about this situation. Three days later, the program director sent out an apology letter to the cohort on behalf of the program.

After a week had passed, Whiteness, as it so often does, revealed itself. Upon returning to class, some White female students tried to excuse their behaviors in the previous class by blaming my colleague for discussing Charleena's murder in the first place. After this exchange, I challenged the students to unpack their Whiteness elsewhere and to speak more respectfully to my colleagues. In response one female student of color and a few White female students confronted the entire teaching team for not modeling "good" pedagogy. Our class fell apart.

My colleagues and I spent the following day reflecting on the situation and decided to each write a letter to the class. Written in the style of a Freire dialogue (2002), I ended each point in my letter with a question that invited all students to write me back. At the start of the next class session, I first sat with students of color, read the portion of my letter addressed to them, and apologized for our team's lack of thoughtful planning on addressing difficult societal issues in class. I then walked to my colleagues, stood by them, and read the remaining of my letter to White students. I pointed out instances of White privilege and racist behaviors. For example, I asked the White students, "Do you treat your White male instructors with more respect based on their racial identity and hierarchy in our college? If so, what does it say about your racial bias against male instructors of color?" I also reminded ALL students that none of them would have the contextual privilege to walk out on their students when difficult discourse occurs in their future K-12 classrooms. I then ended my letter with this question, "You are asking me and my colleagues to teach you through a humanist approach. But are you treating us like humans, imperfect humans?"

Iftikar and Museus (2018) stated that AsianCrit is a useful framework to examine and emphasize Asian Americans' agency in resisting White supremacy and fighting for social justice. By apologizing to students of color, I modeled how to take responsibility for mistakes and embodied agency to lead the class forward. By challenging White students to examine their racial bias, I refused to placate Whiteness and demonstrated my stance on social justice. By reminding ALL students of their professional and ethical commitments to future students, I cautioned students of color to not "play up" Whiteness by seeing themselves only as victims, and encouraged White students to continue unpacking their own Whiteness. In retrospect, I wonder if I were not a first-generation Chinese male immigrant and college student, would the class dynamics have been different? Would I approach this situation differently? And ultimately, would I be treated with more respect and grace?

Counterstory III: Paving the Way Forward

After learning this difficult yet rewarding lesson, I was determined to become an even more caring, concerned, and responsive teacher educator. I continued to take classes with senior and junior scholars in the field of equity, justice, and diversity; attend professional conferences to learn different teaching approaches; and engage in conversations with my advisor, and peers about challenges and possibilities. With the "studying up," I updated the syllabus for the Multicultural Education course. I also negotiated with the program director to assign two colleagues, a Black male international student from East Africa and a Queer White woman from the Pacific Northwest, to co-teach the class during Summer 2018.

Part of the work that summer included centering race and culture in class. I did this by merging my personal stories with professional pedagogies to challenge White students to reflect on how the STEP regularly privileges their voices and experiences in classroom discourse. I asked, with my teaching partners, how ALL students can disrupt this racial hierarchy in the program and their future workplace. Using creative assignments such as "Multicultural Identity Bag," I encouraged students of color to nourish their ethnic heritage, reflect on their contextual privileges, and learn to do the same for and with future students of color in K-12 schools. Sharing my "testimonio" (Cruz, 2012) as an immigrant educator of color with ALL students, I illustrated the challenges of working in urban schools, the rewards that come with the challenges, and the fight I (we) cannot give up yet. My commitment to multicultural education has paved the way for the students I have taught to do the challenging yet necessary work in K-12 schools.

At the end of the course, our team received mostly positive, constructive feedback such as the one at the beginning of this chapter. There were, however, a few racist comments targeted toward me and my Black colleague. For instance, a student wrote, "Cancel the class or shorten it. Instructors need to learn the difference between nice and caring." Instead of taking such remarks personally, I realized that this was an opportunity for the program administrators to "see." Hence, I synthesized and presented the feedback at the next faculty meeting. I acknowledged all the hard work that many faculties had done during the first quarter to help ALL students develop racial literacy; shared the positive feedback that affirmed the value of the course; and read the racist comments as they appeared on the evaluation.

ALL faculties were silent after hearing those comments. Subsequently, discomfort and tension arose from the silence. Shortly, a White male tenured faculty said, "Lin, thank you so much for being so vulnerable in sharing the feedback with us. I don't think I'd be as brave as you are." I responded, "Professor, thank you for being so open listening to the feedback. I hope, with this information, STEP will learn to be more careful about whom to admit." Through these bold and strategic moves, I affirmed the values that first-generation college students of color bring to TEPs; rejected the emasculated racialized stereotype imposed upon Chinese male immigrants (Leong, 2012); and demanded the program make structural changes reflective of its professed values.

Despite my efforts, toward the end of my employment in STEP I became increasingly frustrated with how racially hostile the program director had become. This led to my decision to not return to STEP and pursue other venues of funding. With the advice from my trusted colleagues, I brought a student union representative to a meeting I called with the program director's supervisor, a White gay man. Besides sharing documented examples of inequities at work, I pointed out to the supervisor,

> You know that men of color are demographic minorities in this profession and it is difficult to recruit us to work in teacher preparation programs. Yet STEP has a track record of losing men of color before their contract ends.

The supervisor quickly replied, "There are many reasons for those men of color to leave the program. There are sides of the story you don't know." I calmly replied,

> Maybe, but there are also sides of the story that I know and you don't. Look where we are at now. I am not even nearing the end of my contract and I no longer want to work in the program. The point is that whatever happened to me and other men of color happened. But I'd like you to allocate more resources to support incoming men of color working in the program and make sure that they have a better experience.

At the end of the meeting, the supervisor asked, "Would you like to have a reconciliation meeting with the program director?" I replied, "No. I have forgiven her in my heart. Now it's up to you to do some training with her to make sure that she will do a better job in the future."

Looking back now, being a first-generation Chinese male immigrant and college student in the STEP has not been an easy journey. But I also know this journey is bigger than me. With the contextual privileges granted to me, I advocated for changes that could help the program become a more inclusive place and pave the way forward for and with incoming first-generation college students and teacher educators of color.

A *New* Vision of Teacher Education

Over the past three decades, there have been increasing calls to diversify the US K-12 teaching force (Villegas & Irvine, 2010). Yet Whiteness remains pervasive in many TEPs as seen from my counterstories. Hence, it is critical for TEPs to become intentional about recruiting, supporting, and retaining teacher educators of color to make a systemically positive impact. I hope my counterstories contribute to understanding the complex intersectionality within the broad category of "first-generation college students," and illustrate possibilities for TEPs to transform teacher education into a *nicer* field. When that happens, a *new* vision can be imagined and the soul of teacher education can be revitalized (Zeichner, 2018).

References

Cruz, C. (2012). Making curriculum from scratch: Testimonio in an urban classroom. *Equity & Excellence in Education, 45*(3), 460–471.

Freire, P. (2002). *Pedagogy of the oppressed* (30th anniv. ed.). Continuum.

Gay, G., & Howard, T. C. (2000). Multicultural teacher education for the 21st century. *The Teacher Educator, 36*(1), 1–16.

Iftikar, J. S., & Museus, S. D. (2018). On the utility of Asian critical (AsianCrit) theory in the field of education. *International Journal of Qualitative Studies in Education, 31*(10), 935–949.

Ladson-Billings, G. (2005). *Beyond the big house: African American educators on teacher education.* Teachers College Press.

Leong, K. J. (2012). "A distinct and antagonistic race": Constructions of Chinese manhood in the exclusionist debates, 1869–1878. In P. Spickard (Ed.), *Race and immigration in the United States: New histories* (pp. 112–130). Routledge.

Picower, B., & Kohli, R. (Eds.). (2017). *Confronting racism in teacher education: Counter-narratives of critical practice*. Routledge.

Sleeter, C. E. (2017). Critical race theory and the Whiteness of teacher education. *Urban Education, 52*(2), 155–169.

Takaki, R. (1998). *Strangers from a different shore: A history of Asian Americans* (rev. ed.). Little, Brown and Company.

Villegas, A. M., & Irvine, J. J. (2010). Diversifying the teaching force: An examination of major arguments. *The Urban Review, 42*(3), 175–192.

Zeichner, K. M. (2018). *The struggle for the soul of teacher education*. Routledge.

CHAPTER 13

Strangers Can Make No Noise

Altheria Caldera

> Yet they move with an authority which I shall never have; and they regard me, quite rightly, not only as a stranger in the village but as a suspect latecomer, bearing no credentials, to everything they have-however unconsciously-inherited.
> JAMES BALDWIN, *A Stranger in the Village* (1984, p. 164)

∴

I place my feet
Carefully unto the sidewalks that outline the meticulously manicured lawn
I am told that an alumni created an endowment worth millions
To maintain
    The landscape
I dare not tread on this wealthy White woman's grass.

I position my big Black body
Neatly into these precise white spaces where portraits of wealthy White men
Frame the walls, signifying their commitment to
To maintain
    The buildings
I dare not make myself at home in these wealthy White men's castles.

For I am a stranger in their village
Genuinely desiring
To be heard
Yet
Deeply hoping to make no noise.

Maintenance.

Studying in the Academic Village

It was my first semester of graduate school at the private primarily white university (PWI) I selected for doctoral studies. The class was Psychology of Thinking and Learning. On this particular night, we were discussing cognitive abilities of pre-school children. A classmate pointed out that children from low-income homes usually begin school years behind children from affluent homes. In response, another classmate added that the Head Start program[1] was designed to help *those* poor children gain the skills they need to begin school prepared to learn. What followed was a deluge of questions from classmates curious about the workings of Head Start and about how to educate *those* children. I sat in silence, wanting to admit my guilt – that I had been one of *those* Head Start children – but not wanting to appear *different* or that I didn't belong. The distant, third-person terms my peers used to speak about children from low-income backgrounds told me that I was likely alone in holding experiential knowledge about growing up in an under-resourced home. Although theirs was sterile textbook knowledge and mine was embodied lived knowledge, which I saw as more real, I dared not speak-up. This created an interesting paradox: though I wanted to be visible, to contribute to meaningful class discussions, I didn't want to be scrutinized or singled-out. I didn't want to make too much noise.

When I began doctoral school, I was already an accomplished professional with nearly a decade of teaching and administrative experience at the community college. Just two years prior, I had won the college's highest teaching honor, the Chancellor's Award for Exemplary Teaching. I *thought* I had a strong sense of self. I knew that I was smart, capable, and ambitious. I was confident that I had earned my acceptance into the doctoral program in Curriculum Studies at this university. While I knew that I deserved to be in graduate school, seated next to my classmates, the question of whether I belonged at the university would be a stubborn one.

Despite my Head Start beginning, or maybe because of it, I was determined to be the ideal doctoral student – to show that I belonged. On my first night of class, I had wanted to look like what I thought a doctoral student at this institution would look like. Confident that I had selected the perfect outfit, I had a friend take a picture of me before leaving for class. I wore a nice dress, matching accessories, and heels – only to be surrounded by classmates dressed in jeans or shorts and t-shirts, and wearing messy buns. Ironically, I, whose goal was to fit-in, stood-out for being extra – for doing too much. Retrospectively, it's evident that my aim was to *not* look like the poor girl who attended Head Start. I had wanted to appear like my peers whose parents were architects, lawyers, professors, and dentists. I did not want to appear to be what Baldwin called *a suspect latecomer*. But clearly, I was *a stranger in the academic village* with a lot to learn about village culture. Without saying a word, I was already making too much noise.

These unsettling experiences in graduate school would continue. One time, a classmate leading a discussion asked us to draw a picture of our family home, the house we grew-up in. I hesitated a few moments before putting pencil to paper. Which house would I draw? The first home I remember – a mobile home that was striped in red or white like a peppermint? The second home, another mobile home, this one longer and newer and located in a trailer park? My third home, my grandmother's decrepit mobile home where we moved when my mother divorced her first husband? My fourth home, an old rent house where I once found baby rats under the bed? My fifth home, another rent house where we moved when my mother couldn't pay the rent at the previous house? The house without running water and with a hole in the front door where a knob was supposed to be. We stuffed the opening with old newspaper. Like many people from poor and working-class backgrounds, we were transient. Our moves were dictated by precarious relationships and financial instability. I knew that whatever home I'd draw would show that I grew-up poor. I drew a standard single-wide mobile home that could've been either of the three mobile homes in which we lived. The classmate leading the discussion asked us to hold-up our drawings for our classmates to see. I felt outed – like everyone would now know that my mom was a teenage mother who didn't finish high school. That our electricity was frequently disconnected. That we filled-up milk jugs with water from the local park. That I often washed my clothes by hand and hung them by the fire to dry. That I wore plain glasses paid for by Medicaid. That my absent father was addicted to crack cocaine, the drug that was pushed into our small rural community in the early 90s. My peers would know that I bore *no credentials* confirming that I belonged at a wealthy private PWI. That I had no legacy here, or any other university.

Working in the Village

Not only was I a student, as a graduate teaching assistant (GTA), I was a university employee. On one occasion early in my first year, I was in the staff workroom making copies or scanning documents at the request of the professor for whom I served as a GTA when a White lady entered the room and told me that the room was for staff only. I nervously explained to her that I was a graduate teaching assistant completing a task for my professor. She replied, "Oh, ok" and quickly turned to leave the room. After this experience, I wished I had a badge to signify my belonging. Without this identifier, I was making too much noise. From this moment on, I was careful about the spaces that I occupied. Evidently, certain spaces were marked for select individuals. With my nappy hair, dark skin, and big body, I did not look the part. The professor with whom I worked, Dr. R., had given me a key to her office with permission to work there any time. Though I appreciated her offer, I decided that I would never be caught in her office alone. I didn't want to have to explain who I was and why I was there. I envied the GTAs who were able *to move with an authority which I shall never have* – the ones who belonged because their racial identity, gender, and class backgrounds were more aligned with the traditional academic. Regardless of my credentials and accomplishments, I felt suspect – trying to maneuver my way from the margins into a world that they'd inherited. As a first-generation graduate student, I struggled to navigate this academic space and to form collegiality with those in academic ranks.

I think that institutions neglect the material and psychological needs of first-generation graduate students. For example, I was selected for a study-abroad fellowship. If I wanted to go, I had to pay for my flight in advance and wait on reimbursement when I returned. This expectation seemed to be a common one, so I didn't raise any questions about where I was supposed to find almost $1700 to purchase a round-trip flight to London. While on this trip, the administrator in charge of the fellowship commented that she wished that she had selected another male student so that the one male on our trip wouldn't feel alone. I wondered if she had given me the same consideration as the lone first-generation graduate student, the only Black student. But as is often the case in the academic village, there's a blindness – whether feigned or genuine – to social class and race. I tried, but struggled, to connect with the other fellows. After all, I had grown-up in communities with people who received welfare and food stamps. Who worked in factories or grocery stores. Who worked in cafeterias and drove school buses. Who cleaned White folks' houses and kept White folks' children. Interestingly, but not surprisingly, the people on campus with whom I had the most authentic conversations were the custodial staff – mostly Hispanic women who mainly spoke Spanish. Though I was preparing for a career that would require me to be surrounded by academics, these women were *my* people.

In those early days, my relationship with Dr. R. was my only true connection with an academic. I had told her about my struggle to feel a sense of belonging at the university, and she had shared with me her own conflicts as a lesbian professor at a Christian university. Despite not always feeling like she belonged, she had carved a space for herself and was a beloved professor. Before long, most people in the College of Education knew me, likely because Dr. R. was intentional about introducing me to her colleagues, taking me to meetings with her, and inviting me to other events. Not only did she allow me to accompany her to events, she encouraged me to speak and promoted my abilities among her colleagues. At a Women's History Month planning meeting, she told the committee that I'd be great at a certain project because I had experience in that area. She, who was already a full-professor with approximately thirty years at this institution, became my validation until my presence alone was enough. But in other spaces outside the College of Education, I continued to experience questions about my role.

In my third year, I was assigned to a work with a new professor, the associate dean of education, after the sudden illness and subsequent passing of Dr. R. One day, she sent her other graduate assistant, Meghan (alias), and me to pick-up books from the library. Meghan and I approached the counter as Meghan explained, "Altheria and I are Dr. L.'s graduate assistants, and she sent us to pick-up the children's books you have on reserve for her." While the librarian stepped away from the counter to gather the books, Meghan moved a few feet away to take a phone call. When the librarian returned, I handed her Dr. L.'s library card to begin checking-out the books. The librarian said, "I can't check them out to you. It has to be Dr. L.'s assistant and nodded in Meghan's direction. I stated firmly, "We are both Dr. L.'s graduate assistants." In this moment, I was reminded that regardless of my previous work as community college dean, my 4.0 grade point average, and my stellar work as a graduate assistant, a Black woman who was a first-generation graduate student could easily be suspected of not having any institutional authority, even with a credential (library card) in hand.

During my last year, I was selected for an assistantship in the honors college, serving as the graduate research assistant for the interim dean, Dr. C. The honors college was housed in one of the nicest buildings on campus and boasted high-achieving undergraduate students who earned top-tier fellowships. Its funding signaled its prestige. Along with Dr. C., I frequently attended events with faculty, administrators, and donors. I never forgot to wear the honors college badge that identified me as Dr. C.'s assistant. I never discussed my background. I did what I was instructed. I went where I was told to go. I worked with care, rarely at ease in these borrowed spaces.

By the time I completed my doctoral program, however, I no longer felt like a stranger in the academic village. I had formed many genuine relationships with peers, faculty, and administrators who I knew for certain wanted me to succeed. In fact, my decision to earn a graduate certificate in Women and Gender Studies (WGST), at the insistence of Dr. R., had led me to a community of scholars that included me and validated my work. They were thoughtful feminists who understood and respected the ways gender intersected with race, class, ability, and more. I was honored when the leaders of this department trusted me to co-teach an undergraduate WGST course during my last year of doctoral studies. When I graduated in 2016, I received many congratulatory wishes from these women.

Final Thoughts

Though I was excited to be invited to contribute my narrative to this anthology, my excitement was coupled with fear. I feared casting a negative light on my alma mater when I truly had a mostly positive experience there. I feared the vulnerability that writing this narrative required. In all transparency, I prefer the safety of silence. But as a critical scholar, I am not entitled to "play it safe." To the contrary, I am compelled to take risks, to examine my lived experiences, and to interrogate the impact of institutional power on minoritized populations. My hope is that my testimony will validate the experiences of others who are marginalized in the academy. Perhaps more importantly, I want academics who value diversity and inclusion to be inspired to implement policies and practices that promote equity.

After graduating with my PhD, I began my current tenure-track professorship determined to create learning environments that are characterized by inclusiveness and belongingness. This should be every institution's aim. As academics, the most persistent question we must ask of ourselves is "How can we counter the marginalization and isolation experienced by minoritized students?" The need to belong, to be accepted as individuals without bias or stereotypes, is a basic human need. It is particularly important for graduate students who do not have a legacy of higher education that this need be met. No matter how much we, first generation graduate students, remind ourselves that we deserve to be academics and that our presence matters, only institutions can ensure that we feel belongingness, that diverse experiences and perspectives are validated. Otherwise, institutions remain racist and classist academic villages, and first generation graduate students remain *strangers in the village who can make no noise.*

Note

1 Head Start promotes school readiness of children under 5 from low-income families through education, health, social and other services.

CHAPTER 14

A Black Girl's Magic Is Often Her Blues

Angela Gay

I blink. Rapidly.
Body is weary // from the change // the charge.
The work. // The carrying.
Hasn't this always been the story // of bodies like mine
Fat Black Nappy-Headed Queers.

My identities // provide context for domination.
This is not justice.
It is business as usual
Playing small, my crucible.
I used to seek respectability
In a disrespected body.
The vulnerability is deadly.
I know.
Taught myself to bury, deep.
Shrink.
Make myself as small // as possible.
So they do not think
me // a threat.

Still // I am visible
fat, Black, and woman
And I am for sale // a commodified body.
My diversity // is used to sell // hopes and dreams
for those who want to be seen // supreme.
Unmarked by the perceived // obscene
unhealthy, immoral, dirty. // Normativity used as bait
I can't tell // who is the prey?
Our mothers // and their mother's mother's mother's pay
Never afforded us // the organic, gluten and sugar free, grass fed, whole foods ...
We // prayed
For sustenance // and are given // substances.

To volatile // for the thin and white.

The balancing of power is precious.

I am supposed to be strong.
Called into service // by institutions
who want me // too meek to raise my voice.
We are lost // balancing a life on the edge
of inclusion // and exploitation

I. Am. // the fucking // other mother.
Everything a delicate balance // when expectations become reality
Full black breasts // wide hips // fed by racism // and apathy
Exorcise my empathy // until
I am empty // and alone
In dorm rooms, // classrooms, // boardrooms
I become // empty and alone
And tired.
So, tired.
... I blink.

Body is weary // from the change // the charge.
The work. // The carrying. // Is hard.
Hasn't this always been the story // for bodies like mine
They say // I choose this lifestyle.
The personal. // The political.
Serving your quotas // teetering a fine line
between representation and tokenism
My sexuality // my Blackness //
Is not your politic // to judge. To convert. To exploit for capital gain.

Do you feel judicious // in the wielding of power?

The crown changes us.
Men and women // disguised as kings and queens
pillaging my body // and my mind // I // am in their sights
A desire for light // in a world of constant night

Sometimes // I am afraid // to close my eyes
The terror // of someone // controlling me
And grounding my flight

This ... is how they almost // conquered the heart // of a Black girl
A fat girl. // A woman. // A human.
A human.
Your toxicity // yields the illusion // of power

And I blink. // I blink and // I blink
Try to regain focus

I blink // for a body // that is weary
From the change // the charge. // the work. // The carrying,
it makes me hard // as stone
stoic // and // hasn't this always been the story
of bodies like mine
History shaping futures // repeating history // of self-seeking behaviors

I // I blink.
People have always tried to tell me // who I am // I blink.
Tried to tell me who I should be // I blink.
And when I didn't listen // they attempted to control me
to conform me // constrict my mind
My body // "Don't wear that"
"It's too short" // "You're too fat."
My eye shadow, "too blue" // "The color harlots wear"

I have never fit in
Too quiet // Too anxious // Too fearful // Too big

Too big.
For these mutha'fuckin desks.
In this grown ass adult space.
Where you tell us we are adults,
but want us to follow, blindly,
like abused children

And like an abused and neglected child
I // I find this space does not fit me
because it does not have to
It was not made to serve me // or embrace me
And, again, // I blink.
From weariness.
Institutions do not change // They charge.

WE work // WE carry.
Hasn't this always been the story // told in the dark // about bodies like mine
Who grew up with towels // wrapped around their heads?
Imagining // long blond hair
skin void of melanin – filtered pictures
Holding breath // losing breath.
Take up less space!
until // invisible
In this institution.
How dare I question?
My voice only relevant // when it serves an interest // not of my own
I am a separatist when I don't.

I // I blink.
Body is weary // from the change // the charge. // the work. // this carrying.
Hasn't this always been the story // of bodies like mine

I // blink.
I thought I had rejected this narrative
And then // *I arrived* // here.

I blink.
the thinkers and doers
Reminded me.
Wanted me to believe
My body // not good enough.

I blink.
My mind // not good enough.

I blink.
I've got to pop. // and drop.
Like // Black womxn,
and femmes
and girls // do. // Have done.
Since birth.

I blink. // work ten times harder.

To avoid smothering.
In an alleyway.
meeting // certain death.

I blink. // Under the weight of institutionally bred inadequacy

And at night. // I blink. // From weariness.
Ask myself whose narrative do I tell?
By being too much light.

Carrying the oppression of
institutions who thrive on the backdoor trade
of bodies like mine.
Am I creating or being created?

I blink.

Epilogue

To write this chapter I needed to conjure from a place of desire, of strength, and of vulnerability. I needed to be deliberate and unafraid. To be, as Audre Lorde asks of us, in the service of a vision that allows for collective liberation, with the knowledge that my freedom is tied up in yours, no matter who you may be.

As a human who believes in the power of connection, it is difficult for me to focus on a singular place within my doctoral journey as a site for exploration. My reflections have always been an exploration of life experiences as I look historically and contemporarily to explore the synaptic connections that make me human. While this piece is an exploration of my journey as a 1st generation fat Black queer femme doctoral student, it is also a pathway for making meaning of the mental and emotional parts also in pursuit of a PhD. Also, in pursuit of healing through research/me-search.

Thus, this poem is an exposition on my fatigue as a human who has balanced multiple hats while navigating institutional power for many years. Blinking is my body's physical response to the exhaustion of having carried too much for too long and it serves as my first indicator when I am not walking in nor owning my power.

I believe every human holds unlimited power. Power to create, power to liberate, and power to evolve and become. However, what many of us know to be true is that even in the most self-proclaimed liberatory-making spaces, the wielding of power can be subverted in ways that structurally marginalize people through dominance. When power is wielded in ways to diminish others through silencing, unequal distribution of resources, and limiting one's ability to live a full authentic life it creates a false binary of the powerful and the powerless. To encourage such a binary is to encourage the oppression of others and that is an act of violence. As a doctoral student and a professional within higher education I have witnessed and encountered not only microaggressions ever present in higher education spaces, but also intellectual theft, the exploitation of trauma for capital gain, the intentional exclusion of voices, the misgendering, and the pandering of guilt to deny the existence of abuse. These actions most often are used to maintain hierarchy within education. I think of them as the master's tools, those which are used to differentiate between those for whom higher education was created and those of us whose ancestors had to march, protest, and in multiple ways give up their lives to enter.

In my life, this resonates as feeling like an imposter when I know I am more than capable. My ethic of care becomes subverted into other mothering. I produce to feel valued and when I rest, I feel guilty. I perform at an optimum in an institution that erases the contributions of people like me and every evening I go home and spend hours reconciling what it means for me to be a part of a system that does not have the capacity to see me fully. I struggle through my own fears as well as other people's fears for me and their fears of me. I imagine futures and I have learned to yield myself grace.

Where I was expected to shrink, I instead expanded, and positioned myself to teach others to take up as much space as possible. When I felt the expectation to exploit personal trauma, I instead created pathways to tell joyful Black stories that unveil truth by pointing to those who enact violence. When I was treated like a diversity quota, I voiced my difference as a reminder of my humanity. When my queerness became a barrier for others, I asserted it as a gift to explore deep meaningful relationships with everyone I encountered. This type of grace and radical imagining is not easy, yet, it is necessary for my own continued liberation and those whom I work alongside. So, I blink.

I blink to regain clarity and vision when I am exhausted, because though my identities count me among the marginalized, I am also a witness and I believe the act of witnessing demands action. While some days action may mean a nap on other days it may mean showing up as my full self and battling against the ingrained supremacy of whiteness by which we've been taught to measure ourselves.

I am thankful for radical traditions and the scholarship of Black feminists, Womanists, and other critical thinkers who have woven in the threads of our scholarship, their humanity. Their work and sacrifices taught me that Black womxn have voices and that those voices can question, create, make meaning, and speak truth boldly. They taught me that the amplifying of voice is one of the most valuable tools in navigating institutional power. Through their work they have allowed me the space to value my experiences and voice as a means to will myself back into existence, especially in places where acts of dominance seek to erase me.

You came here to create reality, not accept it. (From the "Secret Language of Light" tarot deck)

CHAPTER 15

A Particularly Ferocious Fire within Me

Ebony N. Russ

Being told no (you can't) creates a particularly ferocious fire within me.

∴

On Class

The first fire-starting *NO* was ignited at an early age with the statement, "people who go to junior college do not become doctors."

I was a young, African American teenager from a working class family who lived in a rural farm town when this statement was delivered to me. The town that I resided in was comprised of seasonal workers, blue collar workers, and white collar professionals. The proximity to the Mexican border provided the town an opportunity to experience an influx of Mexican immigrant workers. Since the town was sparsely populated, all children attended the same elementary school, middle school, and high school. The beauty of the lack of educational options placed children from various socioeconomic statuses in the same school system and provided a rich environment for children from these varying backgrounds to have access to similar educational experiences. My peer-to-peer interactions were quite favorable. While in school, I was involved in marching band member, cheerleading, was voted the first black homecoming queen, and many other social, academic activities. My academic experience was fun and rewarding. I enjoyed school; many of my peers; friends; and extended family members in this community.

After the high school sophomore year is when students uniformly began very serious college preparation activities. I was just as excited as my classmates that were children of white collar professionals about college preparation; I was excited to share my collegial aspirations with all who would listen. As a young investigator/researcher, I knew it was important to approach educational and counseling professionals about how to pay for college since that was a major concern for me. During a meeting, with a high school official, I was quite anxious, nervous, and excited; it was a roller-coaster of emotions as I knew I would go to college but was not quite sure how to pay for it. It seemed like a ton of money. I shared my financial concerns and my aspirations to become a pediatrician as well as a list of the colleges and universities with the professional. The white, female education professional assertively exclaimed, "People who go to junior college do not become doctors." This message was delivered without additional context as to why and was followed with "what do you think about becoming a teacher or maybe a nurse?" Remember, I lived in a community where individuals knew much more than you would like about your family and personal life. This was extremely difficult to negotiate as a 17-year old child who lived in a small, farm town, where members of the community all knew the comings and goings of every neighbors' day-to-day lives. This, in fact, to me, felt like a very personal attack on the character of 17 year-old black girl who lived *across the tracks*. My insight gained from this declaration of my disqualification from the white collar labor market was that I, in fact, did not have access to the necessary amount of money, capital, or coin needed to obtain, purchase, and access a doctoral degree because that was meant for *others* not for "struggling" and working class folks.

On Race

The second fire-starting *NO* was provided by a white male supervisor who presumptuously exclaimed, "You can't get a PhD, you can't even write a 'proper' work email."

While working at a mid-sized university located in the South. I was employed in a department where individuals were hired for their "uniqueness," however when that "uniqueness" was displayed in the office; it was ridiculed. During a performance review, I was overly critiqued on emails that were sent at 3 am after working constant 60–75 hour work-weeks, along with my peers, which had become the standard work schedule for this department in order to remain employed. My supervisor knew about my doctoral aspirations and quickly included his unsolicited opinion on my writing capabilities as it relates to future academic endeavors. Throughout my performance review, the white male supervisor presumptuously exclaimed, "You can't get a PhD, you can't even write a 'proper' work email." This declaration of my disqualification as a writer was delivered to my mid-twenty year old self, who recently matriculated from a writing intensive Master's degree program and was well on her way to completing a second Master's degree. Within the double Master's academic experiences, I was awarded multiple merit-based scholarships, grants, and fellowships alongside a well-decorated academic record and work history, all of which was hinged on my communication capabilities. The insight I gained was that I did not adhere to the Eurocentric notion of professionalism in the workplace within the context of this specific white, male's personal biased supervisory lens.

On Gender

The third fire-starting *NO* was delivered by a male professor who blazingly bellowed, "ma'am, the only reason you passed this significant examination is because I could not fail everyone, so be glad you actually passed."

On a surface-level, this academic environment was one that would have been perceived to be quite supportive given the intersection of race, class, and gender of the students, faculty, staff, and employees of this institution. However, discrimination has an insidious nature. As a student, I appreciate challenging coursework and anything mathematical in nature is quite motivating. However, my feminine exterior to some proved that mathematical rigor could not be intellectually stimulating for an individual such as myself. This ill-conceived notion that girls cannot "do math and science" permeated my academic experience on several occasions.

While meeting with a male professor during office hours regarding a grade dispute, I was blazingly informed, "ma'am, the only reason you passed this significant examination (which required a particular statistical skill set) is because I could not fail everyone, so be glad you actually passed!" For this course, there was a departmental and historical understanding that male students, at times, haphazardly approached the same subject matter as female students and received higher academic marks. This declaration of my disqualification as a math and science scholar was delivered with no regard for my pristine academic record, and consistent competencies in both math/statistics and science. The insight gained was that the math and science educational gap for women is real and is completely gender-role based.

∙∙∙

The fire starting "no's" were a painful part of my success story. Without the no's I would not have this particularly ferocious fire of which I manifested so many negative responses into so many resounding and transformative "yes" phases such as: I concur; congratulations, agreed, without a doubt. Additionally, I would never have heard breathtaking affirmations received from notable mentors, scholars, faculty, supervisors, colleagues, students, patients, friends, family members, and self.

The way I conceptualized my experiences is hinged on my current position in society. In order to understand my position in society, I used these conversations as a means to explore how individual characteristics and experiences can be quite impactful and/or traumatic, but how the unique intersection of our identifies make and shape how we experience the world. I am not one dimensional; I am multifactorial and issues exists in a multifactorial plane. The interaction of my oppression by race, class, and gender is not unique, but has uniquely positioned me to disclose my story as to tool to encourage others to defend their dreams at all costs.

The level of personal insight gained from pushing through these *no's* developed a woman who lacks the need for continual validation within in society designed to destroy and dismantle her dreams. The fuel received from dispossession, discrimination, and marginalization have manifested into a high quality, productive, and caring black woman scholar whose particularly ferocious fire has not extinguished.

These three conversations among others help reveal the power of words and the intense effect discrimination may have on how we choose to navigate life. I would not credit these oppressive instances as influences of my success; however, I would include these conversations as tools to challenge my persona and self-worth. These conversations along with many other experiences were powerful because they were intended to be destructive. But the opposite occurred, these foolish attempts to dismantle me instead ignited a fire and perpetuated a spirit of advocacy, reform, revolution. Rather than allowing cumulative negative experiences shape you, use these the negative experiences and shape them into useful resources to add to your life's journey toolkit.

Words are powerful and I hope my words are powerful and encourage those who may have experienced similar situations. I hope these words challenge you to depersonalize oppression from you and move a spirit of courage and hope into you.

Heavy Lifting

No, you can't: WARM
No, you're not good enough: HEAT
No, you're not a good fit: COALS
No, Black girls don't do that: EMBERS
No, may I speak to the supervisor: CHARRING
No, do you work here: COMBUSTION
No, they were a better fit: FLAMES
No, can I touch your hair: FIRE

No, reserve your emotions: FLAMES
No, you should smile more: BONFIRE
No, we regret to inform you: SEARING
No, how many kids do you have: INFERNO
No, this is outside of your skillset: DEVOURING

A Weighted Bar

Yes, I am: PEACE
Yes, I know: HARMONY
Yes, I won: ORDER
Yes, we have received your submission: REALIZATION
Yes, you have been accepted: WELL-BEING
Yes, congratulations!: HOPEFULNESS
Yes, you've been selected: STRENGTH
Yes, thank you for listening: SELF-EFFICACY
Yes, you are amongst the top: SUCCESS
Yes, and the winner is …: MATURATION
Yes, top scholar is …: ATTAINMENT
Yes, my name is.: COMMUNITY
Yes, your name: PROSPERITY
Yes, our names: SAVVY
Yes, looking good, Sis!: HAPPINESS
Yes, meaningful relationships: ASCENDANCY
Yes, greetings Soror!: ZEAL
Yes, she is the Therapist/Scientist/Professor/Doctor/Lawyer: ADVANCEMENT
Yes, you are the 1st: TRIUMPH

CHAPTER 16

This Is Soul Work: A Portrait of Three Black First-Gen Docs

Jason K. Wallace, Raven K. Cokley and Lamesha C. Brown

> If there is a book you want to read but it hasn't been written yet, then you must write it.
>
> TONI MORRISON

∴

Education scholar Dr. Bettina L. Love, emphatically states, "we who are dark want to matter and live, not just to survive but to thrive" (Love, 2019, p. 1). We deserve to live in our fullness, own our narratives, and bring pride to our ancestors. When we began @FirstGenDocs, a virtual space connecting first-generation doctoral scholars, we longed for a space to be centered. We needed a site to commiserate around our comparable struggles and celebrate our individual and collective brilliance. We desired a platform that would not only connect us as first-generation doctoral scholars, but serve as a space that honored our intersectional identities. We created this space because *we*, Black first-generation doctoral scholars, were seemingly absent from scholarship and institutional praxis. Thus, in the spirit of *Sankofa*, we purpose this work for people like us, in an effort to move tenaciously towards our collective liberation.

This chapter borrows from the theoretical foundations of nkwaethnography (Dillard & Bell, 2011), an African-centered ethnographic research approach, and counterstorytelling to explore the narratives of three Black first-generation doctoral scholars who are consistently impacted by multiple systems of oppression and further marginalized due to our first-generation status. We offer our personal encounters with oppressive systems and monoculturalism, the elevation of a singular epistemological position (Gusa, 2010), at a historically white institution (HWI) in the deep South. We conclude by discussing our platform, @FirstGenDocs.

Jason's Story

"I'm just waiting for the day these people figure out that I'm not supposed to be here." This thought echoed in my mind throughout the first year of my doctoral program. I assumed that my university required our faculty to admit a certain number of employees and, since I was a full-time employee at the institution, surely I was the pity pick. Perhaps the need for diversity landed me in the program. As a Black, queer, first-generation doctoral student from a working-class background, I was constantly unsure of my abilities. The lack of representation of those who held my intersecting identities, in both media and the academy, suggested to me that I was not enough.

I was doing something that my family members and friends had not done before, and I had few people to talk with about this process. A few of my white co-workers completed doctorates, but as a Black man, I never felt comfortable asking white people for anything for fear of being perceived as inferior. Besides, their experiences would be completely different than mine, anyway. I only knew a few Black people who were doctoral students or had completed their doctorate, but my pride would not allow me to approach them. Therefore, I had many unanswered questions. I felt like my institution did not know that people like me, Black first-generation students, existed. The institution did not offer any interventions (e.g., discussion groups, workshop(s), resources) pertaining to my first-generation identity. The mere acknowledgement would have meant so much; yet, the feeling of invisibility was overwhelmingly isolating.

It was not until I met other Black first-generation doctoral scholars that I started to feel like there was a place for me. I always felt supported in my Blackness from the community of Black students within my program. However, it was not until some of us discussed our identity as first-generation students that I began to feel seen. The pressure, isolation, and feelings of otherness consumed each of us. As Black students at an HWI, commiserating around our racial identity occupied much of our time. It is difficult for Black students at HWIs to have the time and energy to focus on other aspects of our identity because we are frequently navigating whiteness. We are constantly advocating for ourselves, proving our brilliance, and, justifying our humanity. This is what it means to be a Black first-generation doctoral scholar – regularly feeling the impacts of our first-generation identity, but only having the time and energy to focus on our Blackness. Unlike our white first-generation counterparts, Black first-generation scholars combat racism, on an individual and systemic level, fighting to maintain our place in an academy not made for us. The access to information and social capital afforded to white first-generation graduate students, by way of their whiteness, is not readily available to Black first-generation scholars.

This leaves us in a quagmire, negotiating between advocating for our racialized and first-generation identity.

Once I recognized the salience of my first-generation identity, it was important for me to find community. It was through the @FirstGenDocs platform that I saw myself. I dared to uncover the impostor phenomenon which plagued my experience and realized that I was avoiding seeking help from my faculty and peers. I began to recognize the anxiety attacks I would have each night before class – the nights where I laid in bed wide awake, afraid of what the next day would bring. Through the @FirstGenDocs community, I began to understand that what I was experiencing was not an anomaly; rather, I was experiencing symptoms from the pressure of trailblazing a new path. The weight of my community was on my shoulders. I wanted to set an example for my younger sister and show society that Black men can earn PhDs, too. I began to recognize and name that my pursuit of a doctorate was not just for me, but for so many others; this is where I found my power.

This degree is for Trayvon Martin, Antwon Rose, Tamir Rice, Nigel Shelby and other young Black boys who police murdered or society systematically disenfranchised, never affording them the opportunity to obtain a doctorate. This degree is for my ancestors who were born into slavery and never allowed to receive an education. This degree is for my mother, the most brilliant person I know, whose knowledge society rarely values because she does not hold a piece of paper for surviving an institution that was never built to value her knowledge. This degree is for my community, my kin, and other Black first-generation scholars. These are the reasons why I feel so much pressure. It is why I held anger and resentment about how difficult this process is for Black first-generation doctoral scholars. For us, this process is not just about writing papers and obtaining publications, but *it is soul work* – unpacking the internal and external voices that say 'you cannot' or 'you should not'– and listening to our ancestors who remind us that we were built for this moment.

As I near the end of my doctoral journey, I still wonder when the faculty will realize that I am not supposed to be here. Not because I am not smart enough for the program, but because this university never deserved students like me in the first place. I am enough. *We* are enough.

Lamesha's Story

Do you know what it feels like to sit in an academic building named after a white man who fervently worked to keep Black students out of your institution? If you are a Black student attending an HWI in the South, you probably do. I attended an HWI, where the total Black student population was approximately 8%. Like many large institutions in the South, my institution did not want to integrate, and fought to remain an all-white school. Since that time, the institution has honored racist white men by naming buildings after them and memorializing the fight to end slavery with an artifact on campus that reframes the purpose of the Civil War, calling it the "war for southern independence."

As a Black first-generation doctoral recipient, who comes from a lower-income background, I received plenty of messages indicating that I did not belong at my institution. In addition to the tainted history that the institution fails to acknowledge, the institution does nothing for first-generation doctoral scholars. Support services are purposed for undergraduate students, as it is at many institutions. Given that this identity is invisible, it is easy to forget that first-generation doctoral scholars exist and may need targeted support services. There is an assumption that first-generation scholars have it figured out once they complete their undergraduate degree and therefore, do not need assistance during graduate school. I can only imagine what it would have looked like to have a support group where I could have not only talked about my experience on campus as a Black woman, but also as a first-generation graduate student. A space where my colleagues and I could have received mentoring from those who had navigated the process before us. Institutional support in this way would have showed me that they really did care about me.

It is no wonder that I questioned whether I could *really* do this thing called doctoral study. Staying up late and waking up early to read, with a never-ending to-do list, was part of the academic process that left me feeling like I was not cut out for my program. Feelings of impostorism seemed ever-present. No matter how much I read or how little sleep I received, it did not matter. The feelings of impostorism did not subside. Even with achieving various milestones, there was always that nervousness and thoughts that maybe the next milestone will be the one that I cannot complete. After successfully defending my first independent research study and spending the summer preparing for my preliminary examinations, I cried before receiving my question on the first and third day of my prelims. This journey brings out the best and the worst in you. I dealt with anxiety and fear and, conversely, experienced pride, excitement, and relief. Many people refer to doctoral studies as hazing due to the "break you down to build you up" process. This was my experience; this journey caused me to question what I believe, who I am, and my purpose.

Though this doctoral journey resulted in several lows for me, there were also highs. It took a while before I felt some validation around my first-generation identity; two years into my program, my co-authors and I founded #First-GenDocs. We realized we had unique doctoral experiences due to also being first-generation. Since our very first Twitter chat, we have grown to having over 5,500 followers, including those who are currently in doctoral programs, aspiring doctoral scholars, and those who have completed their doctorate. Not only do I have my co-founders, but I have a community of #FirstGenDocs across the world.

Conversely, I always felt validation within my racial identity. When I started my program, there were so many Black people – particularly, Black women. It was quite affirming for me to be in my classes and see so many people who looked like me. Though my program is well known and highly ranked, I believe that this high number was because #WeRetainEachOther. Within Black communities, this idea that we take care of each other is prevalent. There is no way that we will see our classmates, who often become family, struggling and not come alongside them to support them. When I was struggling, it was my Black classmates that I leaned on; these connections were a huge part of my persistence through the process.

Additionally, I experienced a sense of assurance from knowing that I am my ancestors' wildest dreams. It was my ancestors who set the tone for my perseverance. Despite being kidnapped, enslaved, beaten, raped, killed, treated as second-class citizens, denied basic human rights, and experiencing systematic oppression by white people for centuries, *we* persevered! It is about remembering this struggle and finding ways to serve others, both within and outside of Black communities. It is about working to create more equitable experiences for all. It is about doing the work that matters, the *soul work*. My doctoral journey helped me to recognize the value of social justice and what I need to be working towards, not just for those who identify similarly to me, but for everyone. It is for this reason, that I remain grateful as a Black first-generation doctoral scholar.

Raven's Story

"You've always loved school; you've always been smart." As a Black high-achieving student, I had become accustomed to hearing these well-intentioned affirmations from my family, both fictive and kin. Throughout my academic tenure, I worked hard, stayed focused, and performed my very best. However, as I started to become aware of my first-generation doctoral student identity during the first semester of my doctoral program, I experienced a shift in my understanding of academia and academic excellence. For the first time in my academic life, being *smart* did not mean that I would succeed.

Given that I was the first person in my family to do this work, succeeding in academia meant that I had to be both smart and resourceful; everything that I did not know before, I had to somehow learn, through trial and error. As a Black first-generation doctoral scholar, my learning process essentially meant "do everything that you can to not have to ask white folks to help you." So, I went to conferences that I could not afford, applied for fellowships that seemed too good to be true, and I did my best to *look* like I had it all together, even when my most basic needs were not being met. I was a full-time student and my program did not guarantee financial support for students; with my full academic load, I had little to no time to work another job. Thus, my Black first-generation doctoral scholar identity meant that I had to *hustle*.

I learned the meaning of hustling from my mom, who is the trailblazer for higher education in my family. While in high school, she earned an associate's degree from a community college and later earned a bachelor's degree from an HBCU (historically Black college and university). After my parents' divorce, my mother earned a master's and continued to raise two small children, on her own. I have her to thank for my abilities to navigate systems that were not designed for me to succeed; her hustle is what has allowed me to pursue my own journey as a first-generation academic. Not only am I blazing a new path, but I am doing it without funding support from my institution. Unlike my white and middle-class counterparts, I could not call home and ask my family to cover my tuition and fees. Having dependable funding would have made all of the difference in my doctoral experience. While I was being encouraged to present at research conferences to "get my name out there," I also needed to know that this process would not leave me wondering about how I would pay my rent or buy groceries for the week, while I waited months for the institution and professional organizations to process my reimbursement.

I have spent much of my doctoral journey feeling that the institution and its systems *betrayed* me. However, as I reckoned with my feelings of institutional betrayal, I also remembered that my Black scholar hustle is ancestral; my paternal grandparents harvested cotton in the Mississippi cotton fields, and my maternal grandparents worked as domestic laborers in the south. I come from a long line of resistant and rebellious Black folks who have survived by making a way out of no way.

For me, making a way out of no way comes in the form of #FirstGenDocs. I wanted to create space for scholars like myself who, despite having family members with college degrees, simply did not know the challenges of obtaining a doctoral degree. I am grateful that Jason and Lamesha hear my voice as credible in this work and allow me the space to share *my* experiences, in *our* community. As such, my work and existence within the academy is much bigger than me. This work is for the Black girls and women that we have lost to systemic injustice, like Sandra Bland, Atatiana Jefferson, and Aiyana Stanley-Jones; this work is also for Naomi Wadler, Mari Copeny, and all of the Black girl activists who fight to ensure that we never lose another member of our beloved communities. This work is sacred and full of Black scholar hustle. *This is soul work.*

We Are @FirstGenDocs

Although we entered this journey thinking we were alone, we leave this journey reminded that our community, our ancestors, and our first-generation family are with us. As Black first-generation doctoral scholars, we do not do this alone. We use our collective skills and talents to navigate institutions that have failed to center our needs, and complete our mission. We founded @FirstGenDocs as a response to not just our needs, but the needs of our community. Through our monthly Twitter chats, we teach and learn from each other to level the playing field for first-generation scholars. Through our virtual writing retreats, we hold ourselves and each other accountable. Through our hashtag, #FirstGenDocs, we laugh together, cry together, navigate our failures, and celebrate our successes. We are living in our fullness, owning our narratives, and bringing pride to our ancestors. We are surviving *and* thriving. Our unity is our power; and we will continue to "affirm the experiences, amplify the voices, and celebrate the brilliance of [Black] first-generation doctoral students" (Andrews, Cokley, & Wallace, 2017, p. 1). We are @FirstGenDocs.

References

Andrews, L., Cokley, R., & Wallace, J. (2017). *#FirstGenDocs*. Retrieved September 15, 2019, from https://www.firstgendocs.com/

Dillard, C. B., & Bell, C. (2011). Endarkened feminism and sacred praxis: Troubling (auto) ethnography through critical engagements with African indigenous knowledges. In G. J. Sefa Dei (Ed.), *Indigenous philosophies and critical education: A reader* (pp. 337–349). Peter Lang Publishing.

Gusa, D. L. (2010). White institutional presence: The impact of Whiteness on campus climate. *Harvard Educational Review, 80*(4), 464–586.

Love, B. L. (2019). *We want to do more than survive: Abolitionist teaching and the pursuit of educational freedom*. Beacon Press.

Index

@FirstGenDocs   11, 119, 121–125, 138

academic job market   66
academics   5, 47, 59, 63, 104, 106
activism   56, 58
advising   45, 51, 52, 66, 69, 70
African American
   college students   54, 57–59, 90, 120, 122
   faculty   10, 92
   men   98, 121
   queer   11, 59, 65, 97, 107, 111, 112, 120
   woman   10, 72
ancestors   16–19, 21, 22, 31, 37, 55, 112, 119, 121, 123, 125
anxiety   44, 64, 75, 79, 121, 122
Anzaldúa, G.E.   88
aspirations   6, 44, 70, 114, 115
assimilation   11, 82

belonging   11, 33, 34, 72, 104, 106
Bourdieu, P.   5, 71

Capps, L.   7
childhood   1, 10, 69
   poverty   42
Chinese-American   68
Christianity   104
classism   3, 5, 60, 64, 83
commencement   3
community
   home   4, 8, 62
   scholarly   7, 73
   student peers   4, 113–125
Community College   43, 44, 60, 102, 105, 115, 124
Community Service   122
courses   44, 57, 71, 90, 93
critical pedagogy   6
critical race theory   25, 76, 77
cultural capital   6, 65, 90
culture   2–6, 10, 20, 30, 54, 57, 59, 67, 80, 84, 93, 97, 103
culture-shock   54

Davis, A.   2

disciplines   2, 5, 20, 21, 30, 60, 62, 64, 86
diversity   3, 38, 85, 86, 93, 97, 106, 107, 112, 120
Dunbar, P.L.   69

embodied experiences   2, 19, 20, 22
emotional labor   5, 52

faculty   4, 5, 7–11, 33, 36, 39, 45, 48, 51, 56, 57, 59, 62, 63, 65, 67, 70–73, 84, 87, 89, 91–93, 97, 98, 103, 105, 116, 120, 121
   mentors   63, 73
family
   distance from   4, 62
   extended   17–19, 54, 114
   income   12, 102, 106
   support   46–48, 53, 70, 87, 90
FASFA   60
Fellowships   9, 46, 47, 68, 104, 105, 115, 124
feminism   2, 58, 85, 106, 112, 116
financial aid
   graduate student   61–65, 68, 69, 71–73, 98, 105, 124
   undergraduate student   5
First Gen Student Supports
   creating support networks   9, 48
   graduate   50
   undergraduate   50, 52

gender   2, 4, 6, 8, 11, 56, 60, 64, 93, 104–106, 116, 117

Harvard   68, 71
help seeking   121
heteronormativity   50, 60–62
heterosexism   9, 10, 60
high school
   academics   5, 43, 53, 61, 106, 115
   college counseling   1, 69, 70
Hill Collins, P.   2, 58
Historic Black Colleges and Universities (HBCU)   9, 31, 34, 56, 57, 124
hooks, b   2, 4, 11, 58, 93
humor   10, 82, 84
hunger   69

identity 2, 5–8, 46, 56, 80, 92, 96, 97, 104, 120–124
  invisible 122
Iftikar, J.S. 96
immigration 17, 20, 22, 93, 95
  undocumented 17, 20
imposter syndrome 5, 11, 49, 57, 63
injustice 8, 60, 65, 78, 83, 125
institutional change
  leading 21
  need for 5
institutional violence 83–86, 88, 112
intersectionality 2, 99
isolation 2, 22, 32, 34, 54, 106, 120

Jaggar, A.M. 6
Jakobsen, J.R. 44

Laotian-American 9, 72
Latina 9, 48, 55
Linkon, S.L. 4
Love, B.L. 119

marginalized groups 59
memory 11, 18–20, 56, 77
mental health 58, 63, 65, 66, 85
mentoring
  graduate 51, 52
  high school 35, 53, 62, 70, 77
  undergraduate 50, 52
Mexican-American 44, 52, 114
  indigenous 44
microaggressions 8, 32, 34, 35, 51, 83–85, 112
Miller, P.J. 6
mindfulness 60, 64
motherhood 46
  single 9, 42–46, 48, 53, 79, 85, 89
multi-lingual 93–95, 97

Native American 85

Ochs, E. 7
online education 90
oppression 2, 3, 8, 11, 17, 20, 60, 64, 76, 80, 111, 112, 117, 119, 123

place 3, 24, 32, 34
poetry 2, 7

Powell, M. 88
power 2, 3, 5, 11, 26, 38, 51, 54, 64, 75, 84, 86, 92, 95, 106, 108, 109, 111–113, 117, 121, 125
praxis 16, 19, 83, 119
preliminary exams 35, 122
predominantly White institutions 9, 31, 34, 56, 69, 73, 79, 93, 119
private education 102
professionalism 83, 116

queer 4, 11, 60, 65, 97, 107, 111, 120

racism 3, 10, 11, 28, 31, 35, 41, 56, 60, 76–78, 85, 86, 95, 108, 120
Reay, D. 4
research
  assistantship 54, 105
  methods 19, 79
    culturally relevant 56
  publishing 58
  questions 8
    questions of legitimacy of research questions 19
resilience 3, 10, 70, 82, 83, 93

Sayer, A. 5, 6
settler colonialism 20, 21
sexism 3, 9, 60, 64
sexuality 2, 6, 8, 61, 64, 108, 198
Skeggs, B. 4
Sleeter, C.E. 93
smart 34, 50, 57, 68–70, 90, 102, 121, 123
social capital 120
social class 2–6, 93, 104
sociology 20, 60, 61, 64, 66, 90
student loans 44, 57, 61, 87, 91
study abroad 104

teachers, K-12 96, 97, 99
teaching
  adjunct 43, 63
  assistantship 24, 54, 61, 91, 105
time 1, 5, 9, 16–22, 24, 26–28, 30–36, 39, 42–47, 49–53, 55–63, 65, 66, 69, 70, 72, 78, 84–87, 89, 92, 93, 103–105, 116, 120, 122–124
trauma 67, 78, 83, 84, 86, 112
Trump, Donald 16, 20

undergraduate experiences 31, 61, 69, 91
unwritten rules of academia 57

voice
  breaking silence 5, 27, 46, 58
  silencing 112

Waters, J. 63
Whiteness 10, 25, 28, 83, 93–96, 99, 112, 120

white supremacy 8, 10, 17, 28, 53, 78–80, 83, 95, 96, 112
work 1, 3–6, 9–11, 16, 18, 20–22, 27, 35, 39, 43, 44, 46–54, 61–63, 66, 69, 70, 72, 78, 82, 88–90, 92, 94, 97, 98, 103–110, 112, 113, 115–117, 119, 121, 123–125
working-class 3–6, 9, 11, 50, 60–62, 65, 89, 90, 94, 103, 120
writing groups 9, 10, 46, 82, 83, 85, 88

www.ingramcontent.com/pod-product-compliance
Lightning Source LLC
Chambersburg PA
CBHW061416300426
44114CB00015B/1960